Race Talk in
White Schools

Race Talk in White Schools

Re-Centering Teachers of Color

Mara Simon and Laura Azzarito

LEXINGTON BOOKS
Lanham • Boulder • New York • London

Published by Lexington Books
An imprint of The Rowman & Littlefield Publishing Group, Inc.
4501 Forbes Boulevard, Suite 200, Lanham, Maryland 20706
www.rowman.com

6 Tinworth Street, London SE11 5AL, United Kingdom

British Library Cataloguing in Publication Information Available

Library of Congress Cataloging-in-Publication Data

ISBN 978-1-4985-9876-7 (cloth : alk. paper)
ISBN 978-1-4985-9878-1 (pbk : alk. paper)
ISBN 978-1-4985-9877-4 (electronic)

∞™ The paper used in this publication meets the minimum requirements of American National Standard for Information Sciences—Permanence of Paper for Printed Library Materials, ANSI/NISO Z39.48-1992.

Contents

List of Figures and Table

FIGURES

TABLE

Introduction

Whiteness is pervasive in educational contexts in the United States, positioning teachers of color as "hypervisible," potentially marginalized, and requiring continuous struggle for social change. The prevalence of Eurocentric curricula and pedagogies that prioritize whiteness in schools engenders students, teachers, and administrators of color as ethnically minoritized "outsiders," calling for the need for a shift to social justice pedagogies within schools (Leonardo, 2009; Solórzano & Yosso, 2001; Ladson-Billings, 2001). The racial demographics of schools indicate a rise in de facto school segregation; schools with balanced populations of students, teachers, administrators, and staff of color and white as envisioned by supporters of the school desegregation movement and the *Brown vs Board of Education* ruling in 1954 are a rarity (Harper, Patton, & Wooden, 2009). However, shared cultural experiences among school community members may lead to a greater sense of fulfillment, meaning, and purpose for teachers of color, along with more positive academic outcomes for students of color (Farinde, LeBlanc, & Otten, 2015; Gay, 2010). Therefore, it is imperative to determine wider means of encouraging inclusion, retention, and longevity within the educational field for teachers of color.

The current state of educational demographics must be considered in order to better understand how to cultivate culturally inclusive schools. The "hard facts/figures" of the demographics of public schools in the United States are important because they frame this book. The disparities across school demographics underscore the need for further analysis on how race and its historical implications have impacted considerations of "normal," valid, worthy, and legitimized standards for teachers and teaching in today's schooling environment. The current public and private school populations makeup illustrate numerous inequalities that highlight just how deeply whiteness is

1

thoroughly embedded within schools. The most telling statistic is that of the teacher population: over 80 percent of public school teachers in the United States are white and female (National Center for Education Statistics [NCES], 2018b). While the overall numbers of Latino/a and Asian and Pacific Island/ Asian American teachers have grown slightly in the past four decades, the number of Black teachers has increased at a much slower rate, meaning that the overall percentage of Black teachers has actually *decreased* in the past-thirty years. Continued highlighting of whiteness in teaching reveals that in private schools, the teacher population jumps up to 88 percent white (NCES, 2017). Over 80 percent of public school principals are white (NCES, 2017). Most institutions of higher education do not have proportional representation of students of color in undergraduate degree programs, since students of color comprise 38 percent of bachelor-degree seeking college students, a disproportionate ratio compared to overall population numbers in the United States (U.S. Department of Education, 2016). Over 65 percent of all graduate students across programs and over 70 percent of all graduate students in the field of education identify as white (U.S. Department of Education, 2016).

Research on teacher recruitment, retention, and job satisfaction predictors designates the need for engaging in a shift of pedagogical praxis toward supporting teachers of color as well as addressing barriers to entering and succeeding in the profession (Renzulli, Parrott, & Beattie, 2011; Rogers-Ard, Knaus, Epstein, & Mayfield, 2013). Given that job satisfaction is a predictor of teacher retention rates, as teachers of color enter and work in predominantly white schools, they are more likely to experience decreased job satisfaction and therefore higher rates of attrition from the profession (Farinde-Wu & Fitchett, 2018). Farinde-Wu and Fitchett (2018) also determined that teachers of color have higher rates of job satisfaction at urban, non-charter schools. This is significant because research on teachers in general (e.g., mostly white teachers) indicates that suburban schools are the location which predicts the highest rates of job satisfaction (Farinde-Wu & Fitchett, 2018). Yet, for teachers of color, being located in a school where they are in the majority, and can "see" themselves among the students, staff, administration, and their fellow teachers, generates greater job satisfaction. However, even as teachers of color experience an enriched sense of fulfillment and commitment to their profession in urban schools, they are still required to align their pedagogy and work for student competencies with local and national standards, which typically match up with white, middle-class norms of teaching and learning. Further, schools as collective entities represent dominant whiteness—the number of schools described as "intensely segregated," or having between 90 percent and 100 percent students of color enrolled, has more than tripled in the last twenty-five years and now stands at almost 20 percent of public schools in the United States (NCES, 2018a; Orfield, Ee, Frankenburg, &

Siegel-Hawley, 2016). Additionally, over 40 percent of public schools report employing zero teachers of color, demonstrating the furthering of school segregation rates within racial lines (National Collaborative on Diversity in the Teaching Force, 2004).

In higher education, there are similar skewed statistics toward those who are "knowledge holders" (i.e., faculty) and "gatekeepers" (i.e., administration) identifying as overwhelmingly white as well as evidence of a dominant hegemony of whiteness which positions faculty and students of color as "outsiders." Faculty within academia are over 75 percent white, with disproportionately higher percentages of white men represented at the full and associate professor levels (NCES, 2018a). Additionally, adjunct, part-time, lecturer, or other non-tenure track positions, which are less stable and less prestigious positions, are held by faculty of color at significantly higher rates than their white counterparts (Finkelstein, Conley & Schuster, 2016). Faculty and students of color located in predominantly white institutions often experience marginalization, isolation, consistent microaggressions, covert or overt discrimination, and oppression in schools where dominant discourses of whiteness prevail (Berry, 2005; Solórzano, 1998; Yosso, Smith, Ceja, & Solórzano, 2009; Yosso, 2002). The culture of academia for graduate students has also been identified as overwhelmingly white and has been identified as one of the factors contributing to a higher attrition rate for graduate students of color (Brunsma, Embrick, & Shin, 2017). In teacher education programs, enrolled preservice teachers in both undergraduate and graduate programs are over 70 percent white (King, McIntosh, & Bell-Ellwanger, 2016; U.S. Department of Education, 2016) and rarely are topics of diversity, racial equity, cultural competency, and racism centered and foregrounded within teacher education programs (Matias, 2013a, 2016; Sleeter, 2001). Existing scholarly literature indicates how teacher educators, or academic faculty within institutions of higher education who engage with preservice teachers, should be responsible for developing awareness within their students of both racial injustice within schools and the United States educational system, along with the value and importance of initiating culturally relevant, sustaining, and disrupting pedagogies (Levine-Rasky, 2000a; Paris & Alim, 2017; San Pedro, 2018).

The above statistics and research indicate that the vast population of key stakeholders in education—teachers, administrators, policymakers, and teacher educators—are white. Thus, the predominance of white ideals, values, and norms in schools has been upheld and reified for decades, although often in invisible ways. The ubiquity, normality, and invisibility of whiteness make it is easy to deny or ignore the ways in which whiteness has grounded education, from current pedagogies, funding allocations, resource distributions, and ultimately, to the disappearance of the teachers of color workforce.

The telling history of ongoing school "integration" attempts, which have, for the most part, failed, reflect white dominance in determining white, middle-class schools as the "norms" and "standards" of education against which all other schools are evaluated.

Informed by district and state guidelines and mandates, schools often employ subconscious or unacknowledged tactics to uphold whiteness within schools and utilize a "deficit" approach to teachers and students of color. A deficit approach means white teachers either disavow or attempt to change the cultural and linguistic practices many teachers and students of color bring to school in favor of practices considered to be superior— those of white families, students, and teachers. This includes, for example, justifying the tracking of students of color, allowing white supremacist and racist teacher beliefs without repercussion, and refusing to address notice-able funding disparities among schools with high numbers of diverse populations (Kohli, 2009; Matias, Viesca, Garrison-Wade, Tandon, & Galindo, 2014; Yosso, 2005).

As it stands now, the low percentages of teachers of color and the absence of culturally relevant and sustaining pedagogies are indicators of the cyclical nature of the teacher socialization process (Gay, 2013). There has been an extraordinarily high number of white teachers in public schools since desegregation efforts began in earnest. This means that for students of color, the teacher education pipeline, from being socialized as students to completing teacher education programs, to entering the field of teaching, is often the product of majority white teachers from start to finish. The cultural disconnect between white teachers and students of color (i.e., future teachers) from a teacher socialization perspective is one informed by whiteness, invisible or structural racism, and approaches to teaching and learning characterized by a "deficit" approach. As such, white teachers hold power over students of color in determining classifications such as "at-risk," "disadvantaged," or "underachieving" (Ladson-Billings, 2014), potentially preventing them from pursuing the field of teaching altogether (Irizarry, 2011). Alternatively, if students of color do opt to enter a teacher certification program, white teachers and teacher educators have informed their understandings of what teaching should mean or look like within the acculturation phase of teacher socialization. Teaching may not be viewed by preservice teachers of color as empowering but rather a profession in which they will endure racialized aggressions and ultimately may leave for another field altogether.

District, state, and national assessments corroborate the assumption that the cultural and linguistic practices of whites are most highly valued within educational contexts by designing and implementing assessments that require student proficiency in these practices (Paris & Alim, 2017). Teachers of color, drawing from their lived experiences, may struggle to conform to the expected white ways of interacting with students, facilitating the construction of knowledge, and ascertaining whether their students have met certain success metrics for learning (Gay, 2010; Ladson-Billings, 2014). The cultural discordancy between the approaches by teachers of color to the processes of teaching and the assumptions of whiteness within standards, assessments, pedagogies, and curricula in schools means that teachers of color may have difficulty achieving "successful" performance ratings by their supervisors (Rogers-Ard et al., 2013). Additionally, teachers of color must navigate racialized assumptions from their white teacher colleagues and supervisors, which is an additional emotional burden and directly impacts their ability to successfully perform their work as educators (Matias, 2016).

Throughout the book, the term "teachers of color" is used in reference (but not limited) to Black, Latino/a, Asian and Pacific Island (API), Indigenous/ Native, and Arab identities because it is an all-encompassing term that highlights the teaching experiences of multiple minoritized ethnic groups. However, it is important to recognize some of the underlying problems with this term. First, on the one hand, it erases the spectrum of colorism identified in the literature that establishes, for example, Black and Indigenous experiences in schools as distinct from API, Latino/a, and further racially marginalized identities (Hunter, 2016; McGee, Alvarez, & Milner, 2016). On the other hand, it maintains whiteness as invisible or normative by ignoring that whiteness too is a racial identity. Second, the description ultimately serves to define populations in opposition to what they are not (white). To counteract this "flattening" of a multitude of racial identities and experiences, specific racial identities are named throughout the book where applicable and possible. Additionally, at times, the language shifts to accentuate the how whiteness constructs people of color as minorities (i.e., "minoritized"), presenting a postcolonial approach that highlights an imposed-upon epistemology. Ultimately, the lack of specific and nuanced language that accurately represents the range of identities and ethnicities located within and across communities of color without conflation and without definition by what they are not (i.e., "nonwhite") illustrates white power dynamics embedded within linguistic construction (Kubota, 2016).

Current scholarship on issues of racial inequality and whiteness in education indicates that little change has ultimately been affected in the past fifty years, in spite of continuous calls by researchers and teacher educators for new ways of conceptualizing and implementing pedagogies and curricula that critically disrupt whiteness (Allen & Liou, 2019; Bryson, 2017; Esposito, 2011; Irizarry & Donaldson, 2012; Kohli & Pizarro, 2016). Thus, the aim of this book is to address the complexity of issues of race and racism embedded within education from an intersectional perspective that advocates for the integration of culturally relevant, sustaining, and disrupting pedagogies. In doing so, this book aims to answer the following questions: How do teachers of color negotiate whiteness and imbalanced power dynamics when located within predominantly white schools? How might education, a field that has both historically valued Eurocentric curricula and operated within a framework of whiteness, instead aim to destabilize a racialized hegemony and move toward pedagogy that recognizes the potential for agency and empowerment? And how can culturally relevant and sustaining pedagogies be utilized as an agent for social change within education and to support and sustain teachers of color?

In order to answer these questions, this book begins with a historical perspective on racial inequality in schools (chapter 1) to establish how whiteness has been maintained as dominant. Given the complicated legacy of whiteness within the teaching profession, to fully comprehend how teaching has evolved into a predominantly white profession, it is particularly important to be cognizant of the history regarding higher education and teacher training programs. Chapter 1 details how racial segregation and desegregation practices have deeply impacted the teacher pipeline, contributing to the historical weight and underlying assumptions of teaching as a white profession that still stands today as a significant barrier to increasing the teachers of color workforce. The *Brown vs Board of Education* rulings in 1954 and 1955, while couched within a narrative of social progress, have instead, over time, been determined to be, in many ways, a step backward for true racial equity in schools. The methods of integration implemented during the post-*Brown* era have been argued, by some scholars, to be a disservice to students, teachers, and administrators of color, as all three populations endured significant changes to their school environment. In particular, the numbers of teachers and administrators of color declined dramatically as a result of integration and have never rebounded (Milner & Howard, 2004).

As a result of the history of whiteness and racism embedded within education, in the decades post-*Brown*, notions of colorblindness took root and are still maintained today in schools, educational policy, and the teacher pipeline. Discourses of whiteness in education support the invisibility of whiteness as normalized within the United States as well as function to create hypervisibility for teachers of color, particularly those who are located in predominantly white school spaces. As such, chapter 2 uses critical whiteness studies (CWS) to destabilize invisible forms of whiteness, including meritocracy, colorblindness, and white privilege. From there, chapter 3 highlights how "racism as structure" is implemented within school contexts, positioning teachers of color as an "other" in contrast to white teachers. According to Bonilla-Silva (2006), racism does not take place as an isolated attack due to the color of an individual's skin, but racism is, in actuality, a structure integrated within various social systems in the United States, such as schools, that upholds whiteness as a "universal truth." This chapter concludes with an overview of critical race theory (CRT), intersectionality, and white interest convergence theory as ways to deconstruct the notion of a loss-gain binary when it comes to working for racial justice in educational contexts (Milner, 2008). An intersectional CRT perspective is useful in revealing how teachers of color are racialized through the centering of whiteness in schools, minoritized in contrast to their white colleagues, and inherently marginalized through performativities of race and whiteness as ideologies (Gillborn & Ladson-Billings, 2010).

In an effort to reveal how teachers of color negotiate whiteness in education, the voices, stories, experiences, and "small teaching episodes" of eight Black, Latina, and Asian female teachers who all work in predominantly white schools are highlighted in chapter 4. This chapter illuminates and validates the ways in which teachers of color have resisted discourses of whiteness by enacting agency within their teaching lives and contexts (Kim, 2001; Kohli & Pizarro, 2016; Rodriguez, 2011). Morrison (2008) conceptualizes the resistance by teachers of color to oppressive regimes of whiteness in the following way:

> [The teachers of color] exhibited an optimistic view of race relations . . . [in spite of] personal knowledge of racism, ignorance, and prejudice. They described past encounters with racism and resulting frustrations because of it. But they did not succumb to it. Their exposure to racism and prejudice had, in fact, shaped their desire to cope with these forces in positive, proactive ways. (p. 22)

Morrison's (2008) depiction of the experiences of teachers of color mirrors many of the teachers' stories in this chapter, demonstrating the crucial role that a sense of agency and a desire to enact social change can play in shaping how teachers of color understand and see themselves. From the historical backdrop of racism and segregation to the theoretical underpinnings of CWS and CRT, the counterstories of the Black, Latina, and Asian teachers presented are indicative of how the teachers utilized their personal experiences of oppression and marginalization to problematize invisible racism, colorblindness, and white neutrality, moving toward an empowered sense of self and demonstrating how they negotiated whiteness on a consistent basis within their predominantly white school contexts (Baszile, 2008a; Evans-Winters & Esposito, 2010).

The Black, Latina, and Asian teachers' narratives highlight the potential for culturally relevant, sustaining, and disrupting pedagogies as a way to support teachers of color in negotiating whiteness within their educational contexts, along with working for social justice and social change. The predominance of white teachers in the field has resulted in widespread approaches to teaching and learning which "demand and legitimize [white] dominant languages, literacy, and cultural ways of schooling . . . Middle-class norms position languages and literacies that fall outside those norms as less-than and unworthy" (Paris, 2012, p. 93). Thus, chapter 6 identifies how the emotional reality of "race work" for *all* teachers illustrates the need for a shift in approaches to pedagogy in order to both disrupt and de-center whiteness as well as make the teaching profession an opportunity for teachers of color to experience self-affirmation through critical emotional pedagogies. Additionally, through the lens of Mara Simon, one of the authors of this book who identifies as a white teacher educator and scholar, this chapter demonstrates how Mara's narrative intertwines with the eight teachers' "race talk." This chapter concludes by suggesting that all teachers would benefit tremendously from culturally relevant, sustaining, and disrupting pedagogies, which could provide the pedagogical skills, appropriate language capabilities, and a critical framework for addressing racial inequity both inside and outside the classroom.

Increasing teacher diversity is often named as one means of disrupting dominant whiteness within education, yet, in order to increase the numbers of teachers of color in schools, it is necessary to acknowledge and explore the experiences of teachers of color in order to better understand the means of both professional success and personal well-being as well as how to recruit more teachers of color to the field (Farinde, Allen, & Lewis, 2016; Ladson-Billings, 2011). While critical scholars have drawn attention to the increased use of both culturally relevant pedagogies and culturally sensitive research paradigms as a way to highlight and legitimate the experiences of teachers of color (e.g., Kohli & Pizarro, 2016; Solórzano, 1998), it is crucial to continue to expand upon these pedagogies and implement them more widely in order to make "visible" the pervasive yet often invisible notions of whiteness and colorblindness that serve as a framework for educational curricula, pedagogies, and policy in the United States. This book presents the argument that there is a significant need for destabilizing whiteness by enacting culturally relevant, sustaining, and disrupting pedagogies as a way to create more meaningful, equitable, and effective school experiences for students and teachers of color whose identities and experiences are habitually denied, minimized, overlooked, or even rejected. Additionally, this book demonstrates how culturally relevant, sustaining, and disrupting pedagogies can be a tool for enacting social justice as a way of dismantling white supremacy in the creation of empowering educational spaces for historically marginalized teachers and students outside a framework of whiteness.

Chapter 1

Whiteness and "Other" Teachers

A Historical View

ABSTRACT

This chapter explores how the legacy of the *Brown vs. Board of Education of Topeka, Kansas* ruling in 1954 resulted in a set of complicated, racialized educational issues that are still unresolved today. The first part of the chapter explores the impact of *Brown* and the resulting school desegregation movement on teachers of color and the surrounding communities. The swift and severe backlash to the *Brown* rulings was a key means of upholding whiteness in education. The second section interrogates the historical legacy of racism in teaching across racial identities, identifying the ways in which various communities of color have been kept separate from whites within educational contexts through legal mandates. Then, the chapter demonstrates how some social justice scholars have defined the *Brown* ruling as an example of white interest convergence applied to education, leading to the disappearance of the teachers of color workforce. The fourth section of the chapter addresses whites' reactions to desegregation policies, which included "white flight" away from neighborhood schools and the emergence of predominantly white private and charter schools. The chapter concludes by discussing how today's predominantly white teaching force is also, in part, maintained by teacher education programs via the historical legacy of the teacher pipeline located within predominantly white institutions of higher education.

Teaching in the United States remains a predominantly white profession while student demographics are undergoing a rapid shift in diversity ratios, which are expected to continue to rise in the upcoming decades (National Center for Education Statistics [NCES], 2018a). The public school student population in the United States is now more than 50 percent students of color

(NCES, 2017; U.S. Department of Education, 2016). Given the change in student demographics, today's test-driven school curricula need to shift toward more critical and sociocultural conceptualizations of education to support the needs of a diverse student population within public schools. In doing so, teaching can legitimate and validate a broad span of learners' ethnic backgrounds, experiences, and cultures while also demonstrating a commitment to a social justice agenda.

Notably, this is not an argument for the standard ideas of a "multicultural education." The concept of multicultural education is not new, but the term is atheoretical, as multiculturalism puts forward a "colorblind" educational perspective on race and whiteness in schools by promoting the idea of "celebrating our differences" (Azzarito, 2009). Multiculturalism is often conceptualized as a way to learn about "other" cultures (e.g., students bringing in food from their racial or ethnic heritage, wearing a traditional clothing garment to teach their peers about its meaning, etc.), thus setting up, maintaining, and stabilizing an "other"/white dichotomy. Several critical scholars in the field of education have recently advocated to move away from a "multicultural" approach, suggesting instead, to focus on critical perspectives that aim to destabilize the "other"/white dichotomy as well as to disrupt imbalanced power dynamics that are a product of school-based racial inequities (Cochran-Smith, 2010; Convertino, 2016; Gay, 2010; Ladson-Billings, 2014).

In order to better understand the current educational climate and identify the roles of race and whiteness within schools, policies, and national or state standards and legislations, it is vital to reference the complex, systematic, and hierarchical history of the intersection of race, social class, and education. Thus, this chapter explores how the ruling and legacy of the *Brown vs. Board of Education of Topeka, Kansas* decision in 1954, often heralded as a landmark case in the fight for social justice, has yielded a set of complicated, racialized issues regarding school segregation and integration attempts or reforms. The first part of the chapter explores the impact of the *Brown* ruling and resulting school desegregation movement on teachers of color and the surrounding communities, including the swift and severe backlash to the *Brown* rulings—a key to upholding whiteness in education. The second section interrogates the historical legacy of racism in teaching across racial identities, identifying the ways in which various communities of color were, through legal doctrine, kept separate from whites within educational contexts. The third section of the chapter demonstrates how, while the *Brown* ruling was framed as intending to achieve racial equality, some social justice scholars have instead defined the *Brown* ruling as an example of white interest convergence applied to education, leading to the disappearance of the teachers of color workforce. The chapter then addresses whites' reactions to desegregation policies, which included "white flight" away from neighborhood schools and the emergence of predominantly white private and charter schools. Both reactions served to maintain de facto school segregation and marginalize teachers of color even further. The chapter concludes by discussing how today's predominantly white teaching force is also, in part, maintained by teacher education programs via the historical legacy of the teacher pipeline located within predominantly white institutions of higher education.

TEACHING FOR "WHITES ONLY": A HISTORICAL VIEW

Since its very formation, education in the United States has been rooted and intertwined with both whiteness and socioeconomic status, and this intersection of social class and race sustained an economy based on the labor of enslaved Black people and then continued with the cheap, exploited labor of many other communities of color (e.g., Chinese and Latino/a immigrants; Godfrey, 2008; Gonzalez, 2013; Milner, 2006). While abolition ended formal slavery in 1865 and labor laws began to provide some protection for workers of all ethnicities, lawmakers quickly enacted national and state legislations that explicitly denied anyone who did not identify as white the means to gain educational advancement as well as financial and societal success (e.g., the Naturalization Act of 1870, the Chinese Exclusion Act of 1882, the Day Law of 1904, the Indian Citizenship act of 1924, and more). These legal processes maintained whiteness at the top of the racial hierarchy and functioned, implicitly and explicitly, to traditionally oppress communities of color through discriminatory laws regarding, for instance, owning property, attending public schools, learning to read, and being able to vote. Those laws, in addition to other repressive dictations, historically prevented specific ethnic and cultural groups from obtaining both individual and group-level economic, political, and socio-educational freedoms. When this historical and legalized backdrop of racism is taken into consideration, it is impossible to conceptualize the future of education without recognizing the role of the legal system and political legislations that have guided and informed school practices and funding sources for many years, intentionally or unintentionally keeping schools, teaching, and learning for "whites only."

As an indirect result of the *Brown vs. Board of Education of Topeka, Kansas* ruling in 1954, standard integration processes continued to center whiteness within education by increasing the number of schools where white women taught students of color within white contexts, rather than providing schools with majority students and teachers of color equal funding and socio-educational resource allocations as well as sustaining and protecting the jobs of teachers of color (Franklin, 1990; Morris, 2001). As such, students, teachers, and administrators of color were consistently measured against the "educational standards" of their white counterparts, and usually were unable to "measure up" for a multitude of social and contextual reasons. Thus, the *Brown* ruling has ultimately failed in its effort to provide equal educational opportunities as school and residential segregation rates continue to rise even today (NCES, 2018b; Orfield, Ee, Frankenburg, & Siegel-Hawley, 2016), and whiteness maintains its hold within education as the "academic norm" to which teachers and students of color must strive to achieve.

Students, teachers, and administrators of color have endured de facto "separate but *not* equal" educational experiences for decades without significant change. Notions of whiteness have been a key factor in how schools, achievement, and learning are understood and constructed. A foundation of this argument is the historical determinations of how, in spite of claims to the contrary, the *Brown* ruling ultimately led to implicitly racialized legislations enacted by white lawmakers which dictated how education was for "white students only." Yet between the *Plessy vs. Ferguson* ruling of 1896, which upheld the idea of "separate but equal" facilities for teachers and students of color, and the *Brown* rulings of 1954 and 1955, many schools of color were able to thrive in spite of a lack of funding and resources due, in part, to highly qualified teachers, along with the cultural congruence between the students, teachers, and administrators (Fairclough, 2004; Franklin, 1990; Siddle Walker, 2000). Schools located in communities of color, along with their teachers, were often considered pillars or anchors of their communities. Social justice scholars have contended that desegregation efforts were ultimately detrimental to the academic success of students of color, and to the middle-class economies for communities of color, resulting in the deep decline in the teachers of color workforce (Milner, 2006; Morris, 2001; Irvine & Irvine, 2007; Karpinski, 2006). In particular, desegregation had a negative impact on the school achievements and sense of self for teachers and students of color, resulting in a slow but rising awareness around racial inequalities in education throughout the 1960s and 1970s (Foster, 1997; Garte, 2017; Kohli, 2008).

In the decades post-*Brown* and as integration began in earnest, students of color did not, as *Brown* had intended, experience desegregated and "equitable" schools with equal access to resources, funding, and support. Rather, students of color were positioned within one of two polarizing educational experiences: either they were located in schools labeled as "underperforming" and underfunded with a high population of teachers and students of color or they were bussed into well-funded schools staffed with predominantly white teachers. This racialized and classed dichotomy of schooling experiences has maintained whiteness as a "mainstream, racist, and hegemonic framework that has consistently questioned the worthiness" (Harper, Patton,

& Wooden, 2009, p. 409) of teachers and students of color, failing to provide equitable educational spaces. Thus, whiteness is still relevant and visible in today's educational landscape via widespread de facto school segregation.

FROM SCHOOL SEGREGATION TO INTEGRATION INTO "WHITE CLASSROOMS" ACROSS RACIAL LINES

School segregation in the United States was widespread prior to *Brown* and was upheld regarding any individual who did not meet the expectations of the cultural codes established by whiteness and institutionalized within state and local districts. It is important to point out the fact that it was not solely Black students and teachers who were excluded from having access to equal education in their own communities. While popular narratives on segregation and integration in education are often characterized by Black individuals (e.g., Ruby Bridges, the Little Rock Nine), such narratives ignore the history and experiences of many other racialized ethnic groups who were also historically excluded from equitable and well-funded educational schooling contexts (Godfrey, 2008; Kuo, 1998; Powers, 2008; Teranishi, 2004). Latino/a, Asian and Pacific Islander, and Native populations experienced systematic discrimination for decades through formal segregation policies enacted in various states and cities across the country. For example, until the practice of segregation was challenged in federal court in 1951, Arizona frequently maintained separate buildings and schools for Latino/a students and teachers, thus upholding the majoritarian story that whites were superior to any racialized "others" (Macdonald & Monkman, 2005; Solórzano & Yosso, 2002). Similar practices of outward racial discrimination occurred for Latino/a student and teacher populations in states such as California, Texas, and Colorado. Yet, in spite of being underfunded and overlooked by their authorizing districts and at the state level, many Latino/a schools were supported by their communities, providing spaces for education where Latino/a students could be taught in culturally congruent and relevant ways by Latino/a teachers (Macdonald & Monkman, 2005). Additionally, Latino/a communities also founded many private schools which hired mostly Latino/a teachers to better support their students when the public school options failed to do so (Salinas, 2000). Latino/a efforts at desegregation toward equitable funding and resources for their schools, teachers, and students resulted in a series of court cases, ultimately leading to the 1947 *Mendez vs. Westminster* ruling, a predecessor of *Brown* and considered to be a major desegregation court case in United States history (Gonzalez, 2013).

In spite of many state-level court challenges to the blatant segregation of Latino/as within educational contexts, whiteness was consistently upheld in each of the rulings as judges applied irregular and socially constructed conceptualizations of race in order to maintain legal loopholes and make outright rulings that reinforced de facto school segregation. By maintaining separate schools across invisible racialized lines, the connections between whiteness and teaching were reinforced through a racial hierarchy where white teachers worked at high-performing white schools while Latino/a teachers were relegated to segregated and underfunded Latino/a schools (Godfrey, 2008; Gonzalez, 2013). The legal system's ongoing reinforcement of school segregation enabled individual school districts to employ calculated means of preserving separate "lesser" schools and classrooms for Latino/as, which often lacked funding and resources, maintaining the distinction of these schools as "less than" their white counterparts with white teachers. The tactics and strategies employed by districts toward school segregation were unnamed but carefully coded within phrases such as "choice," "freedom," "classification," "student transfer," and "ability," thereby making it difficult to challenge since the processes which resulted in school segregation were not explicitly stated but rather implied or formally unspoken and not mandated (Godfrey, 2008). Additionally, after the *Brown* ruling, the legal construction of Latino/a citizens as white meant that school districts could still uphold de facto segregation by placing a few Black students into "integrated" schools with white teachers and arguing that they were following orders to desegregate while still maintaining school segregation where most Latino/as attended separate schools.

As a result of residential enclaves (e.g., "Chinatown," "Little Korea," etc.), various Asian and Pacific Island (API) American subgroups have also historically experienced de facto school segregation, through the effects of long-term discriminatory laws that prevented API immigrants from obtaining citizenship or owning land, such as the forced internment of Japanese Americans during World War II (Teranishi, 2004). The high rates of residential segregation within API populations often resulted in neighborhood schools consisting of almost entirely API populations, including teachers. Those schools with predominantly API students and teachers were typically poorly funded and overlooked by local and state district leaders (Rong & Preissle, 1997). For example, in San Francisco, Chinese Americans were originally prohibited from attending all public schools and then, when this law was struck down by the state court of California and in an upholding of the "Separate but Equal" doctrine of *Plessy vs. Ferguson*, Chinese Americans were ultimately segregated into Chinese-only schools with Chinese teachers (Kuo, 1998). Far more explicitly racist, Native populations were systematically and forcibly taught by white teachers in segregated schools with the explicit goal of extinguishing Native culture, traditions, and identity (Grant & Gillespie, 1993). Native populations are also severely underrepresented within the teaching force due to the structural barriers of whiteness embedded within teacher education programs which promote Eurocentric ideals and fail to address Native people's experiences of cultural genocide, discrimination, and systematic dehumanization (Locke, 2004).

While school segregation is often framed within the context of Black/white race relations, as history and legal studies have demonstrated, the often de jure separation, exclusion, and marginalization of various racialized groups reflected white policymakers' managing control over the teaching population, maintaining white teachers as the "norm" as well as control of resources such as money, property, education, and language (Godfrey, 2008). Over time and after the *Brown* ruling, policymakers have instead employed de facto school segregation as a strategical means of preserving whiteness as the dominant culture in public schools. Such strategic means included, for example, inequity in resource disbursement between whites and ethnic and racially marginalized groups, the racialized stratification of teaching populations, and the disappearance of teachers of color. Thus, it is clear from a historical perspective how many policymakers, administrators, and educators have envisioned teaching as a white profession across race and cultural borders and that teachers of color have experienced the negative impacts of both de jure and de facto school segregation.

THE BROWN RULINGS, WHITE INTEREST CONVERGENCE, AND THE DISAPPEARANCE OF TEACHERS OF COLOR

School segregation has been the subject of much civil rights protest and political or social action, eventually leading to the *Brown vs. Board of Education* ruling in 1954. The *Brown* ruling is publicly revered as a high point of societal progress in the United States toward racial equality, commonly discussed and analyzed in textbooks and history or law classes, and is frequently used as the basis of the argument for a colorblind educational perspective. According to many policymakers, administrators, and educators who espouse this perspective, the work of addressing and dismantling racism was established by this ruling over sixty years ago and therefore no longer necessary. *Brown*'s resulting intentions to desegregate are imbued with the idea that racially balanced schools should be the main overarching goal of equal education for all and that simply implementing this idea will automatically facilitate equity (Morris, 2004). However, while the case was initiated from an altruistic position, the resulting outcomes of the *Brown* ruling ultimately have not been entirely positive in terms of enhancing educational equality, equity, and social justice (Ladson-Billings, 2004; Yosso, Parker, Solórzano, & Lynn, 2004).

While the *Brown* ruling is often associated with the inherent "goodness" and natural order of the social and civil movement for racial equality, the result of this ruling partially reflected an anti-Communist rhetoric to sustain the United States' image as a world leader of democracy in line with its Constitution (Donahoo, 2006). This was particularly relevant to the historical time period, given the contentious relationship between the United States and several communist regimes in the years leading up to the Cold War. Several social justice scholars have argued that while the case was framed and presented to the public as intending to achieve racial equality stemming from social understandings of racism and the desire for a greater common good, the *Brown* ruling actually represents an example of white interest convergence (Ladson-Billings, 2004; Bell, 2004). For instance, Ladson-Billings (2004) suggested that white judges, lawmakers, and stakeholders realized that in order to protect white interests, which included "improving the national image, quelling racial unrest, and stimulating the economy" (p. 5), the reversal of *Plessy vs. Ferguson,* or the "separate but equal" ruling, was necessary to maintain and protect white interests and white privilege. The *Brown* ruling, along with another series of cases on school segregation which are known as the *Brown II* rulings of 1955, came down to end school segregation but the language was vague, nondescript, and lacked a specific time frame, all of which provided numerous legal loopholes and allowed individual state and local districts autonomy in determining exactly how to interpret and implement the ruling (Donahoo, 2006). In the decades after *Brown,* schools with high populations of teachers and students of color experienced reductions in funding, worsening conditions without means for improvement, and a lack of qualified teacher applicants. This resulted in schools that employed predominantly teachers of color facing economic hardships, sociocultural ostracism, and a dearth of educational resources to be able to meet the achievements and requirements of the national and state standards set by white policymakers. Further, the required academic achievements reflected white terms and were based on the success of white, middle-class schools as well as the effectiveness of white teachers (Kohli, 2008).

Reactions to the *Brown* ruling resulted in significant white resistance and backlash to the idea of school integration, including negative white reactions and white opposition to the enforcement of policies intended to promote equality or disrupt imbalanced power dynamics (Hughey, 2014). For example, The Citizens Council was immediately formed after the decision was handed down, a group characterized by white, upper-, and middle-class segregationists (Andrews, 2002), and chapters were established throughout the South in an effort to prevent school desegregation through legalist tactics. Much of the white backlash to not only the *Brown* decision but many other legislations and court cases which intended to provide some measure of educational equity to teachers and students of color were a result of the misconception that their success could only come at the expense of white schooling resources. The notion that the limited nature of existing resources must be "protected" from use by teachers and students of color created a polarizing oppositional dichotomy of whites versus communities of color. This dichotomy was constructed upon the false assumption that teachers and students of color were coming to "take" all the resources from the white teachers and students who had worked hard to "earn" the fruits of their labor in the form of economic, social, and political gains (Andrews, 2002; Donahoo, 2006; Fairclough, 2004). Because of public support and the overt nature of the backlash and resistance to integration, many individual schools and local districts openly refused to integrate and accept teachers of color into their schools, or were purposefully slow in making any institutional changes, sometimes waiting a decade or longer to address the *Brown* rulings and subsequent requisite desegregation efforts (Milner & Howard, 2004).

While schools were required to desegregate post-*Brown*, the ruling in 1955 gave a tenuous timeline for desegregation, simply noting that schools should engage in the process "with all deliberate speed" (Ladson-Billings, 2004, p. 5). The lack of a distinct or definitive timeline within this ruling meant that it could be interpreted on an individual basis, which effectively slowed desegregation down tremendously as schools, administrators, and district officers tepidly began the integration process but often dragged their heels to implement any official, formal, or actual changes (Donahoo, 2006; Yosso et al., 2004). Another obstacle to formal integration efforts was the obtuse wording of the *Brown* rulings. While, on the one hand, the ruling clearly condemned racialized school segregation, on the other hand, the wording avoided providing specific or intentional mandates and directions to state or local districts. Additionally, prior challenges and rulings to inequitable segregation practices were never ordered to be revisited by local courts or actually implemented by schools, meaning that the individuals from cases which had served as the early forerunners of the *Brown* rulings never even saw justice. In other words, parents, teachers, and administrators of color who took risks by challenging the dominance of whiteness within a specific school setting and won their legal case often, even with their legal victory, were still not granted admittance to their desired educational institution or saw any immediate impact on vastly unequal segregated educational contexts. For example, while the *Sipuel vs. Board of Regents* case in 1948 ruled in favor of the plaintiff, agreeing that the Black female student who brought the suit had been discriminated against, the court then refused to grant an order guaranteeing her the right to enroll in the school (Donahoo, 2006).

Upon reviewing the long-term effects of *Brown* more than sixty years later, it is clear that this ruling was deliberated upon and delivered by whites who, even with potentially good intentions, were invested in protecting white interests, upholding whiteness at the top of a racialized hierarchy within schools and education. Specifically, the *Brown* rulings failed to consider two important issues: first, integration did not directly facilitate equal education for *all* students, especially in public school communities with a significant cultural discordancy between teachers and students. Second, the ruling dismissed and ignored all the schools with teachers of color that were successful in educating their students of color and were playing a key role in supporting and sustaining their broader racially minoritized communities (Fairclough, 2004; Foster, 1997; Morris, 2001, 2004; Powers, 2008; White, 2002; Siddle Walker, 2000). The notion that students of color should be brought into white schools, leaving teachers of color behind, reflects the idea that school curricula driven by whiteness were considered superior over all other racial identities, and stand as the "academic standard" of achievement for *all* teachers (Foster, 1997). In other words, simply integrating, or placing students of color into white schools with white teachers and maintaining that this integration would provide "equal" educational experiences, aimed to protect white privilege and white norms in schools. However, locating students of color alongside white students and white teachers within the same school building in white communities did not translate into providing "equal" education for *all*. Importantly, this also meant implicitly and explicitly disavowing and/or excluding teachers of color from schools, revealing how the initial "good" intentions of constructing a more equitable educational system via the *Brown* ruling ultimately protected whiteness as the norm in public schools.

Not only was the familiar imagery and rhetoric of desegregation, for example, Black students being bussed into white school districts, not problematized until decades later, but the idea of "flipping" or "reversing" these desegregation methods was *never* considered. If integration was truly the goal of the *Brown* rulings, then the reverse, such as white students bussed to schools serving communities of color, should also have occurred. But, in spite of the fact that, for example, Black teachers were often very well-trained and even outpaced their white counterparts in demonstrating competency and commitment within the field (Ladson-Billings, 2004; Siddle Walker, 2000), schools and courts never suggested "reverse" integration. Notably, the seemingly ludicrousness of reversing traditional integration efforts of bringing students of color into schools traditionally reserved for white students illustrates the underlying intentions of whiteness embedded within the *Brown* desegregation efforts toward educational "equality." Desegregation clearly was not necessarily intended to establish both equalizing educational access and balanced diverse student and teacher populations within *all* schools.

Rather, desegregation resulted in providing limited and unequal access to the socio-educational and economic resources for schools with predominantly teachers of color while prioritizing resources for predominantly white schools and maintaining the dominance of a white teaching force in place (Milner & Howard, 2004). Moreover, the unanticipated consequence of this approach to integration resulted in job loss for teachers of color in their own school communities, thus excluding teachers of color from public schools in the movement toward desegregation (Foster, 1997; Morris, 2001).

The Civil Rights Movement, "Second Class" Teachers, and the Loss of the Teachers of Color Workforce

While the *Brown* ruling is portrayed in history books and in classrooms (i.e., educational contexts) as a pinnacle of the civil rights movement and one of the founding means of achieving racial equality, this was not reflected in the experiences of many teachers of color. For instance, teachers of color who found themselves in integrated schools faced significant resistance to their presence and their teaching capabilities from white teachers, students, and administrators. Teachers of color were forced to endure a challenging, unwelcoming, and hostile teaching climate and faced the material consequences of racial discrimination and injustice (Foster, 1997; Bell, 2004). This was in sharp contrast to schools where teachers of color had worked prior to integration, where they experienced professional success and were a source of pride within the schools, and wider communities (Carter, 1980; Bell, 2004; Love, 2004; White, 2002; Siddle Walker, 2000). Although schools in communities of color were often ignored by white governing school boards or district leaders, the teachers in these schools were committed to the education of the students of color who attended, uplifting, educating, and supporting their own communities (Morris, 2001, 2004). However, as districts began to implement integration policies which solely focused on placing students of color into white schools, many successful schools located in communities of color were forced to close due to the loss of attending students. This meant a significant job loss for teachers of color, and thus the disappearance of teachers of color from public schools (Foster, 1997; Irvine & Irvine, 2007).

The movement for school desegregation did not originate from the struggles and hopes of teachers of color for equality as many of them recognized the potential for job loss from resulting integration policies and enactments. In the years leading up to and immediately following the *Brown* rulings, smaller and less powerful local and state teacher professional organizations raised concerns about the potential impact of *Brown* for on job loss for teachers of color (Fairclough, 2004). For example, many states created and implemented laws which allowed for the dismissal of Black teachers if they openly supported

integration or were associated with organizations who worked for integration (Karpinski, 2006). However, larger national groups such as the National
Association for the Advancement of Colored People (NAACP) ignored these
concerns and pushed on with their quest for integration, arguing that it was a
necessary cost of the work toward more equitable school systems and society-
wide social justice outcomes (Fairclough, 2004).

In the immediate two decades after the *Brown* ruling, the rate of job loss
for teachers of color increased significantly, due, in part, to the legal system's
refusal to address or decry formal segregation policies of local school boards
(Etheridge, 1979). This was one material and consequential effect of the *Brown*
ruling on teachers of color. As teachers of color experienced increased rates of
firing or job demotions, and subsequently tried to push back against administration decisions by going to court, judges often viewed the teachers of color
as inferior and refused to interfere with schools' decisions regarding teaching staff appointments and firings (Etheridge, 1979). Other anecdotal reports
claimed that post-*Brown*, there were widespread firings of teachers of color,
Black teachers in particular, were fired "for nothing" or in retaliation for supporting educational equity organizations, thus cultivating a legacy of fear and
inadequacy for Black teachers and teachers of color (Fairclough, 2004; Foster,
1997; Karpinksi, 2006; Morris, 2001). For example, while in May of 1954,
there were almost 82,000 Black teachers employed across the country, in the
decade immediately post-*Brown,* an estimated 38,000 Black teachers lost their
jobs (Etheridge, 1979). The numbers of principals and administrators of color
were also greatly reduced, particularly in southern states (Karpinski, 2006). In
North Carolina, for example, the number of Black principals declined from
227 to 8 between the years of 1965 and 1970 (Karpinski, 2006). However, the
exact numbers regarding job loss for teachers and administrators of color on
a national level are difficult to pinpoint due to a lack of accurate recording of
national data on teachers (Etheridge, 1979; Tillman, 2004).

Not only was the loss of teachers of color devastating for students of color
and for public schools, but this also had a noticeable impact on the wider
communities within which the schools, students, and teachers were located.
For example, Black teachers and administrators were often highly visible
and well-regarded members of their communities, living and working among
their students' families, and representing a significant portion of the middle-
class population within these communities (Tillman, 2004). But after desegregation efforts began in earnest, students and teachers of color experienced
a shift in this way of life as percentages of both populations were moved
into white schools, where they were positioned as outsiders or considered
"less than" their white counterparts. The rapid and widespread loss of jobs
within communities of color due to desegregation implementation wreaked
economic havoc on middle-class populations within the communities,

destroying one of the economic "building blocks" which supported many of the social systems in place (Karpinski, 2006). In addition, many schools in communities of color were either shut down or consolidated and absorbed by white schools, thus requiring teachers of color to work in predominantly white schools. When moved to white schools, teachers and principals of color were often demoted (e.g., going from a head teacher to a classroom aide, from a principal to a classroom teacher, etc.) and demoralized by working in their new white school contexts (Fairclough, 2004; Foster, 1997; Milner & Howard, 2004). As a result of the implementation of desegregation efforts, many teachers of color lost their esteemed community status as culturally competent educators who formed meaningful and impactful relationships with their students when working in "their" schools. Instead, teachers of color who maintained employment but were re-zoned to white schools often faced overt or covert racism or a hostile working environment as well as a loss of professional respect and personal meaning for their position within their school and their communities (Milner & Howard, 2004; Tillman, 2004).

The closing of schools in communities of color, the firing of teachers and administrators of color, and the placement of students of color into white schools all served to maintain a racialized hierarchy within schools rather than creating equal educational opportunities for *all* students. Further, according to Yosso et al. (2004), desegregation efforts were a "disruptive and often violent process" (p. 10) for communities of color. The *Brown* rulings lacked guidance or required mandates on how to put in place structural changes in schools and school or district policies toward equality and integration to enhance an equitable schooling system for *all* students. The notion of desegregation simply meant that students of color were dislocated, moved into a new physical location, tracked within white schools, and often placed into remedial or special education classes (Irvine & Irvine, 2007). For teachers of color, desegregation efforts meant either losing their jobs altogether or becoming "second class teachers," either by working in more and more segregated and often poorly funded schools in communities of color *or* by being denigrated as an "other" teacher if working in predominantly white schools (Foster, 1997; Milner & Howard, 2004; Morris, 2001).

DESEGREGATION IMPLEMENTATION AND "WHITE FLIGHT" TO CHARTER OR PRIVATE SCHOOLS

The *Brown* rulings and resulting attempts at integration meant that many white parents refused to have their children attend desegregated schools, and thus started looking into alternatives for schooling. White parents' resistance to desegregation meant a significant uptick in private school enrollment,

particularly in the South, as well as in the implementation of new district policies such as "school choice" or the creation of charter schools (Andrews, 2002;
Renzulli & Evans, 2005; Li, 2009). In particular, white parents' response to
integration was "white flight." The term "white flight" as an unintended but
long-lasting consequence of integration policies refers to patterns of white
people's movement to maintain de facto segregation in many aspects of their
lives, from housing to schooling to employment and more. As an example,
researchers identified a significant decline in white students for schools that
had a population of students of color above 30 percent (Renzulli & Evans,
2005). In response to desegregation, many white parents started to move
their children to predominantly white schools, resettle into predominantly
white neighborhoods, or enroll in white charter or private schools (Clotfelter,
2001). Not only did a surging increase in white flight in the decades following
the *Brown* rulings yield both overt and covert resistance to school integration
efforts but the loss of taxable income from a significant population of the
middle- and upper-class tax brackets had a detrimental impact on schools
with predominantly students and teachers of color. While these latter schools
were often already underfunded and ignored by the governing municipalities,
"white flight" withdrew even more funds from the tax base supporting local
school infrastructures.

In addition to migration patterns of home buying, social justice scholars
have also identified the increase in charter school enrollment and the reliance
on school choice policies as other forms of "white flight" in maintaining de
facto school segregation (Renzulli & Evans, 2005). While national demographics indicate that charter school populations represent more balanced
racial demographics (NCES, 2018b), when placed within local and state
contexts, these numbers show that charter schools are *either* serving almost
entirely white students *or* almost entirely students of color. Since there are
strong lines drawn among teacher segregation rates (i.e., teachers of color
are concentrated in schools with mostly students of color), rarely are charter
schools with predominantly white teachers actually contributing to school
desegregation efforts. Instead, many charter schools serve as a means of
upholding student and school segregation. While policymakers attempted
to create school choice policies to allow parents to select the best option
for schooling to meet their child's individual needs, these types of policies
exacerbated existing educational inequality. In other words, school choice
policies allowed many white parents to "choice" out of diversified schools
into "higher ranked" schools with better funding and a higher population of
white students and teachers (Renzulli & Evans, 2005). This version of "white
flight" from local public schools to alternative schooling options such as charter or private schools, along with "choice out" policies, is a result of white
parents' perception of the "threat" of "others" (i.e., students of color) imposed

by integration, and their effort to maintain white values, privilege, and high social status. Thus, as Amos (2016) pointed out, parents' determinations of private or charter schools and/or school choice was a racialized response to forced desegregation mandates and resulted in the opposite intended effect, as school segregation rates have actually increased over the past several decades and continue to rise.

Alongside charter schools, private schools played a major role in maintaining school segregation in spite of integration efforts, as white parents have opted to send their children to predominantly white private schools (Reardon & Yun, 2002). This is particularly relevant, given that attendance at private schools often requires a certain level of financial or economic privilege and many historically marginalized and/or oppressed racial and ethnic communities in the United States experience statistically higher rates of poverty than whites. As Reardon and Yun (2002) emphasized, the predominance of private schools is mostly racially segregated, giving white families with economic means the opportunity to continue to self-segregate into white majority educational contexts. The increase in white enrollment at private schools in the last fifty years is important to understand as it has historical significance and is directly tied to school integration efforts based on the *Brown* rulings. For example, in the South in the 1960s and 1970s, a series of private "segregationist" academies opened with the primary purpose of keeping white students out of desegregated schools. In 1975, these private academies enrolled over 750,000 students in total and in some states such as Mississippi, over 20 percent of white students attended private white academies (Andrews, 2002). Privatized education such as these schools were initially supported by state or local governments and infrastructures as a means of avoiding integration, using state tuition grants, and public facilities for free or reduced cost, receiving or transferring educational materials from the public school system, and providing tax deductions (Andrews, 2002). As a result, the overall number of students who enrolled in private segregationist academies jumped to 10 percent of the white student population nationally by 1980 and has continued to increase ever since, providing the basis for a statistical analysis of this segregationist process, or the racialization of schooling. As Reardon and Yun (2003) argued, Black students' presence in public schools, especially in the South, is still an influential factor in white parents' decision to enroll their students in alternative (i.e., white) private schools. The impact of these white segregation academies has resulted in the clear delineation of private schools as white spaces for students *and* teachers. For example, Jackson, Mississippi's private school sector was recorded as over 85 percent white in 1998 (Reardon & Yun, 2003). This number clearly illustrates the segregationist underpinnings of these elite white academies that originated with the aim of keeping white students away from students of color and increasingly marginalizing teachers of color. Thus, in spite of the *Brown* ruling and subsequent integration attempts, the increased enrollment of white private schools serving majority white students has been a significant factor in maintaining de facto school segregation.

Researchers have evidenced that racism and de facto school segregation rates are inextricably intertwined, and that the *Brown* rulings, while characterized as intended to achieve some form of racial equity within education, is yet a long way off from implementing an effective social justice agenda in education (Bell, 2004; Donahoo, 2006; Irvine & Irvine, 2007; Orfield et al., 2016; Yosso et al., 2004). As anti-racist scholars and educators have argued, whiteness is still embedded within education, and the history of desegregation and white flight becomes salient as a way to pinpoint how whiteness is pervasive in today's pedagogy, practice, and policies of schooling. As teachers of color have either slowly disappeared or are concentrated in schools serving communities of color (Raible & Irizarry, 2010), integration efforts toward equality have yet to yield more racially equitable public school contexts.

Desegregation Efforts, Public Policy, and Teacher Education

Teaching in the United States is a predominantly white profession, as more than 80 percent of teachers identify as white and female, and over 40 percent of schools report hiring *zero* teachers of color (NCES, 2018a; National Collaborative on Diversity in the Teaching Force, 2004). National, state, district, and school policies, white administrators, and white educators all play a significant role in maintaining social control of education. The history of teaching in the United States, rooted in whiteness, is also linked, in part, to teacher education and teacher preparatory programs via the teacher pipeline, typically located within predominantly white institutions of higher education (Farinde, LeBlanc, & Otten, 2015). The current demographics of teaching as a white profession are the result of desegregation efforts stemming from the *Brown* rulings that had the unintended consequence of decimating the population of teachers of color. Between schools that served communities of color losing student attendance and subsequently closing, leading to job loss for teachers of color, to the firing or demoting of teachers and administrators of color (e.g., Black principals were almost entirely demoted to classroom teachers), along with the increase in gatekeeping at institutions of higher education that prevented college students of color from attaining teaching degrees, the *Brown* rulings ultimately resulted in a significant decrease in the number of teachers of color (Arnez, 1978; Morris, 2001; Foster, 1997; Irvine & Irvine, 2007). For example, Irvine and Irvine's (1983) review of literature provided substantial evidence for their argument that traditional desegregation methods were detrimental to the Black teacher population. In a follow-up review, the researchers found that since 1980, the number of Black teachers had decreased by almost 50 percent, clearly showing the devastating effects of desegregation (Irvine & Irvine, 2007). Etheridge (1979) documented how very little data on the attrition rates for from the field for teachers of color were maintained during the first wave of desegregation efforts immediately post-*Brown*.

To better understand how current de facto segregation within institutions of higher education (i.e., the lynchpin of the teacher pipeline) has taken concrete forms in today's schooling, it is useful to examine the historical conditions that have impacted the evolution of racism within educational contexts. For example, in contrast to schools today, where the vast majority of teachers are white regardless of individual school student demographics, prior to the *Brown* rulings, many students of color were taught by teachers of color (Foster, 1997). In particular, as part of the after-effects of Reconstruction efforts, Black educators spent decades pre-*Brown* in segregated schools honing their craft as a professional endeavor and cultivating respect for teaching within their communities (Karpinski, 2006). Many teachers of color were trained at some of the best teaching institutions in the north (e.g., Teachers College Columbia University or University of Chicago), making them even more qualified to teach than some of their white counterparts. Notably, because the *Plessy vs. Ferguson* ruling decades earlier established the legality of "separate but equal" doctrines, teachers of color were, at the time, often formally and legally prohibited from teaching in white schools. Teaching as a profession was highly desirable in many communities of color: for example, over 60 percent of Black college graduates pursued a teaching career versus 20 percent of white college graduates at the time of the *Brown* ruling (Karpinski, 2006). Black communities, especially in the South, had a clear and understandable preference for Black teachers to work in Black schools due to underpinning notions of Reconstruction. Black communities used teacher congruence as an "affirmation of racial solidarity" (Fairclough, 2004, p. 4) as they navigated freedom from white rule (Milner, 2006). For example, in 1952, over 85 percent of Black teachers were college graduates, because teaching was a valued profession in Black communities and an important and appreciated pathway to financial stability and upward social mobility (Karpinski, 2006). Within segregated educational contexts, teachers of color teaching students of color in schools located within their own communities created a sense of belonging and positive support for students and their families (Fairclough, 2004; Garte, 2017; Ladson-Billings, 2001; Siddle Walker, 2000).

While the decade after the *Brown* rulings that overthrew *Plessy* as unconstitutional paved the road for school desegregation, however, teachers and administrators of color experienced significant job loss and demotions that continue to have a tremendous impact on today's teacher demographics, showing teaching as an almost entirely white profession (Harper et al., 2009; Karpinski, 2006, Morris, 2001, 2004; Irvine & Irvine, 2007). As a result of desegregation, teacher homogeneity took shape over time and continues to be strongly visible in today's public schools (Ladson-Billings, 2004). After *Brown* and through desegregation efforts, as teachers and administrators of color were dismissed, white teachers were expected to educate students of color in schools that maintained whiteness as the dominant ideology, teaching in a learning environment that often discriminated against students of color (Kohli, 2008).

The *Brown* rulings ended formal and overt school segregation, but this did not automatically result in equitable schooling environments for students of color. Instead, often covert or "invisible" policies were brought forth by lawmakers and school districts that maintained status quo de facto school segregation. For instance, the *No Child Left Behind* (*NCLB*) act, in effect from 2001 to 2015, did not explicitly name race as a motivating factor but maintained whiteness as superior in school contexts that are well-funded, dictating both school curriculum and means of assessment of student learning to ensure accountability. Leonardo (2007) stated that *NCLB* was a national policy informed by centuries of educational legislation that aimed to "strengthen and solidify" whiteness rather than attempting to reveal it and disrupt it. The language in this policy embraced a neoliberal discourse of individual achievement while simultaneously failing to recognize historical and structural inequities that positioned students of color as "deficient," labeling historically oppressed student populations as "underachieving" "underperforming," or "at risk" (Leonardo, 2007, p. 263). Given that teachers of color are a missing force in today's public schools, especially those in predominantly white communities, but more likely to work in racially marginalized, "underperforming," and underfunded schools, this legislation did not support but rather was detrimental to sustaining teachers of color.

NCLB specifically intended to improve the academic progress of four historically marginalized groups of students: students of color, students with disabilities, economically disadvantaged students, and students who are English learners. Yet what is unacknowledged within the language of the policy is the idea that *NCLB* gave "whiteness the license to declare students of color failures under a presumed-to-be-fair system" (Leonardo, 2007, p. 269), and implicitly condemned the pedagogies of teachers of color who work in schools that predominantly serve communities of color. When schools with diverse student populations did not meet the standards of whiteness set forth by *NLCB*, the schools, teachers, and students were characterized as "failing" the standardized tests, and moreover, teachers held as primarily responsible for the lack of success. This colorblind approach to a one-size-fits-all standard of accountability maintained predominantly white and middle-class schools as the model of success on the one hand, and penalized schools and teachers in schools that serve communities of color with failing student performances on standardized tests, on the other hand. While *NLCB* laid out educational standards for success as "neutral" or "unbiased," however, standardized testing represents powerful discourses of whiteness that implicitly punished, with severe financial penalties, the schools and teachers located within socioeconomically disadvantaged and diverse communities (Leonardo, 2007; Orfield et al., 2016). Thus, *NCLB* as an educational policy intensified the struggles and hurdles for teachers of color to be considered "successful" by white norms and standards since their students were failing standardized assessments. Passed more than sixty years after the national movement to equalize education through the *Brown* ruling, the *NCLB* act highlighted the long-term effects of both de jure and de facto school segregation that have ultimately preserved whiteness as the status quo within schools. Since formal segregation policies are no longer enacted in the United States post-*Brown*, policymakers have subsequently put other strongholds into place in order to maintain white dominance and superiority within education and educational policy.

Teacher Education Programs as "Gatekeepers"

Teacher education programs within institutions of higher education are one means of "gatekeeping" within the teaching profession that set up certain criteria to determine who is accepted to become a teacher and who is recommended as qualified to teach. Racialized inequality, prejudice, stereotypes, and biases are major factors historically embedded within the gatekeeping process of higher education, informing who is allowed into the teacher pipeline and who emerges successfully. The gatekeeping within the teacher education pipeline means that many students of color who desire to become teachers are denied entry or blocked from the profession due to processes such as, for example, high-stakes teacher certification standardized testing or being placed within a predominantly white school for student teaching.

Scholars have criticized teacher education programs as lacking in teacher candidates of color, failing to recruit teacher candidates of color, overemphasizing the importance of classroom management and control of students (particularly for urban students of color), and being unable to cultivate white teacher candidates' in-depth critical understanding of racism and culturally relevant pedagogy (Raible & Irizarri, 2010). Since the vast majority of teacher educators (e.g., faculty at institutions of higher education) are white, preservice teachers of color who are admitted into teacher preparation programs often must navigate the white pedagogical and curricular norms and standards of their professors and programs (Gay & Kirkland, 2003). Other means of maintaining whiteness within the teacher pipeline and teacher preparation programs in institutions of higher education include eliminating teacher certification programs at colleges that serve mostly communities of color, and evaluating teachers based on the results of standardized tests such as the National Teacher Examination and General Record Exam (Tillman, 2004).

Similar to elementary and secondary school segregation, higher education (and the teacher preparation programs located within) has a long and racist history of establishing whiteness as the standard for achievement and success. Examples of how de facto segregation within institutions of higher education has been maintained even post-*Brown* include

> the steady underrepresentation of students [of color] at predominantly white institutions (PWI); continued over-reliance on racially-biased college entrance exams; consistent attempts to dismantle affirmative action; increased statewide admissions standards for public postsecondary education without corresponding advances in public K-12 schools; reports of racism and negative experiences for students of color at PWIs; low male student of color persistence and degree attainment rates; forced segregation of historically Black colleges and universities (HBCUs); inequitable funding for HBCUs; and the decline of need-based federal financial aid. (Harper et al., 2009, p. 398)

Considering these examples, the current absence of teachers of color from the profession reflects how policies, laws, and "gatekeeping" have implicitly yet effectively maintained a racial hierarchy within and around PWIs. Further, many HBCUs are often considered less-prestigious "second-tier" schools, in spite of the quality of education students receive, along with the importance of being located within a community that supports their academic outcomes, cultural identities, and social endeavors. Alternatively, students of color who choose to attend PWIs are consistently questioned about the legitimacy of their presence within higher education and their intellectual capabilities (Harper et al., 2009).

Examples of white dominance within higher education in the United States can be identified as far back as the eighteenth century, where formal institutional policies at colleges and universities expressly forbid the acceptance of Black students. In 1833, Oberlin College in Ohio became the first institution of higher education to have a policy that dictated admission to applicants of color. Over the next few decades, propelled by the end of the Civil War, the emancipation proclamation, and Reconstruction, the first HBCUs began to be established. These institutions of higher education were created in an effort to raise the devastatingly low literacy rates among Blacks, but their curricula were usually tightly controlled by the white missionary groups who typically funded the creation of the schools. Whites' control over the funding and curriculum of HBCUs is an example of how the presence of faculty of color within higher education contexts in the United States stems from a white view of what is valid and important within teaching and learning, as well as how white gatekeepers historically have determined funding and policy implementation with white interests in mind (Harper et al., 2009).

The addition of many state-governed HBCUs by the 1890s (versus the private HBCUs established prior) afforded more opportunities for students of color to pursue higher education. However, the focus on agriculture, mechanics, and industry at these institutions—all disciplines that were considered to be "trade" occupations with lower status than many other fields of study—also upheld segregated notions of schooling. HBCUs, particularly state-run HBCUs, were considered less-desirable institutions, provided with less resources and funding, and allowed whites to keep segregation as formal policy (Harper et al., 2009). Even as they were underfunded, the number of HBCUs overall increased after the *Plessy* ruling of 1896, supported by white policy and lawmakers as an implicit yet effective way to maintain segregation within institutions of higher education. In response to the initial challenges by students of color to explicit whites-only policies during the era of legalized school segregation, HBCUs were offered up as an example of "separate but equal" schooling opportunities, meaning desegregation was "unnecessary" according to opponents. However, while the legal doctrine of *Plessy* mandated all public school contexts must be equal in terms of the educational experiences for students, state HBCUs consistently were underfunded and de-prioritized within state and national legislature and budget allocations. This maintained systematic inequality within higher education for students of color at those institutions. Additionally, the very limited presence of students of color within white colleges and universities considered to be more academically rigorous and of higher quality ensured the long-term hierarchy of whiteness within higher education as preeminent and prominent (Harper et al., 2009).

Legal challenges to formal segregation policies in the 1930s and 1940s (e.g., *Pearson vs. Murray; Missouri ex. rel. Gaines vs. Canada*) attempted to utilize a liberalist argument that presented segregationist determinations as failing to uphold the Equal Protection Clause of the 14th Amendment. These challenges were successful because the courts ruled that one state may not rely on another to educate its citizens. This meant that the practices of, for example, offering out-of-state scholarships to students of color to attend other schools rather than integrating existing schools or creating new graduate programs within state limits, were ruled as unconstitutional (Donahoo, 2006). The consistent challenges to school segregation within higher education by students of color in attempts to achieve equal access to education (e.g., *Sipuel vs. Board of Regents, Sweatt vs. Painter, McLaurin vs. Oklahoma State Regents*) were often resisted by white school administrations, who found ways of working around court orders instead of actively desegregating their institutions. For example, in response to the mandated entry of Black students, the University of Oklahoma in 1950 created selective seating sections for Black students within the classrooms, the library, and the cafeteria, thus ensuring that white students would not have to interact with any of the admitted Black students (Donahoo, 2006). As each case challenged the segregationist policies of institutions of higher education under the *Plessy* ruling of separate-but-equal, slowly, those cases started to make inroads toward desegregation at institutions of higher education.

In conjunction with historical landmark events such as the *Brown* ruling in 1954, the signing of the *Civil Rights Act* in 1968, and the signing of the *Higher Education Act* of 1968, many PWIs eventually began to desegregate, thus opening more higher education opportunities for students of color. This process faced immediate backlash by individual institutions and local or state governments, the members of which expressed aversion to the idea of integrating. For example, in 1956, Louisiana passed Acts 15 and 249, which effectively barred Black students from attending many PWIs. These two laws required a certificate of "good moral character" for any Black student who desired to enroll in a public institution but any teacher or administrator who wrote one of these certificates or provided "any other assistance that helped to promote racial integration at any educational level" could be legally fired (Donahoo, 2006, p. 296). Many of the subsequent court rulings on challenges to university and college segregation policies at places such as Louisiana State University and University of Florida theoretically condemned these policies and ruled that these institutions were required to integrate. However, judges in these court cases never actually mandated admittance for the individuals who brought the suits and thus, plaintiffs were never provided the opportunity to actually enroll in their desired programs. This pattern mirrored what was happening within public secondary schools during this time period, with legal loopholes and covert legislation which ultimately worked to ensure that schools at all levels would never be truly segregated, or even close to it.

After lawmakers passed the *Civil Rights Act*, some institutions of higher education began to formally and legally put into practice policies, often known as affirmative action plans, which aimed at integrating student populations in the hopes of addressing the vast divide of racial inequities and prejudices within colleges at the time (Yosso et al., 2004). The *Brown* rulings paved the way for affirmative action policies, engendering a national movement aimed at "equalizing" education through desegregation without recognizing the potential damage of placing students of color into white educational spaces. This led to the development of the term "affirmative action," which came into play in the late 1960s with a further intention toward equalizing higher education access for *all*. Yet from the time of its inception, white candidates who were denied admission to their desired institution have challenged affirmative action policies that were implemented to reserve a certain number of spots for students of color in PWI.

The *Bakke vs Regents of the University of California* ruling resulted in the original upholding of affirmative action and is still referenced today, more than forty years later, as a white man challenged his admission denial to UC-Davis' medical school with the argument that this policy violated the *Civil Rights Act's* prohibition of formal discrimination based on race (Yosso et al., 2004). The court's ruling on this case was twofold; while a 5-4 vote determined that quotas for admissions based on race violated the *Civil Rights Act*, a secondary decision called the Powell Compromise concluded that race could be one of many factors taken into account in the creation of admissions policies intended to facilitate equal access to education within institutions of higher education, particularly PWIs. The Powell Compromise argued that the intention of such policies should be to aim to remedy or address the historical roots of racial discrimination which have prevented access to higher education for students of color. However, the policy of affirmative action has faced continuous challenges, fostered resentment, and potentially even maintained racial inequality. This is because many students of color who occupy a place in PWIs are viewed by whites as having gained access *only* through affirmative action and not through merit-based admission, regardless of their credentials.

The calls to end affirmative action illustrate the powerful roots of whiteness located within notions of meritocracy that have been the basis for whites' argument in their effort to challenge these types of policies. The idea that all students should have an "equal" chance at being admitted into an institution of higher education fails to acknowledge how the economic, legal, political, and educational systems in the United States have been historically set up to maintain whiteness as dominant while simultaneously refusing equal access to resources for students of color. Thus, there is no "equal playing field" or solely merit-based opportunities for students of color to access institutions of higher education, particularly prestigious ones, because they were designed and maintained predominantly for whites. Additionally, external barriers within social and economic forces in the United States also prevent access and represent much higher hurdles for preservice teachers of color. By refusing to recognize the very structural means in which preservice teachers of color are not provided with "equal" opportunities to attend well-regarded institutions of higher education, challenges to both affirmative action policies and the right for students of color to enroll in PWIs altogether ultimately uphold whiteness as the standard through the myth of "meritocracy."

CONCLUSION

As this chapter shows, a number of social justice scholars have interrogated and identified how whiteness within education reifies racial hierarchies; and moreover, how teachers can disrupt such hierarchies, investing in a more culturally relevant curriculum that centers and accounts for the cultural knowledges, understandings, and experiences students bring into schools (Levine-Rasky, 2006; Paris, 2012). Because whiteness is most often centered and constructed as "normal" within schools and enacted by white teachers through "hidden curricula" and by state and national lawmakers as well as district policies (Ladson-Billings, 2001; Leonardo, 2007), it is difficult to name or identify because of its invisibility yet omnipresence. Guided by *Plessy vs. Ferguson* and Jim Crow laws, educational policy has historically functioned as a means of upholding white identity politics and white nationalism within the United States (Leonardo, 2007). Institutions of higher education have enacted gatekeeping processes to maintain segregation, even if it is now de facto rather than de jure, such as it was prior to desegregation efforts. Even after the *Brown* ruling in 1954 and the passing of the *Civil Rights Act* in 1968—both policies that intended to enhance educational equality—schools continue to be informed by underlying discourses of whiteness. The often unconscious or unrecognized desire of white policymakers, school administrators, and teachers to preserve the power differential which reifies whiteness as the standard in education has historically impacted schooling, and thus resulted in teaching as a predominantly white profession. This is still true today.

While the *Brown* rulings have been given status, space, and prestige in U.S.American history books as landmark decisions in the fight for racial equity, the reality and long-term effects of this case had a devastating impact on communities of color. What the history of school desegregation post-*Brown* has demonstrated is how integration efforts were initiated on white people's terms (Fairclough, 2004). In spite of the increasing diversity of the student population in public schools, the *Brown* ruling has resulted in a progressive marginalization of teachers of color within the educational landscape of the United States. The decimation of the teachers of color population, through mandated moves into white schools, mass firings, and implicit assumptions regarding the implied "deficiencies" of teachers of color as professionals, had long-lasting culminating effects, leading to the current low rates of college students of color pursuing teaching careers. This is the reality of today's public schools. Teachers and preservice teachers of color know that their history, culture, and social norms are neither valued nor centered or legitimated in many school contexts with a predominantly white teaching population.

Overall, it is clear that the educational system in the United States, from preschool to graduate school and all the stakeholders, gatekeepers, policymakers, educators, and students within, is one that is defined and normalized by whiteness. Teachers of color are rarely supported within educational contexts and when they are, it is usually based on white interest convergence (Bell, 2004). Examples of white interest convergence includes the historical white missionary involvement in the establishment of HBCUs, the means of enacting of (de)segregation legislation without federal guidelines or support, a lack of legislated federal and state budgetary support for HBCUs, and the gradual reduction or abolishment of affirmative action (Yosso et al., 2004). Further, the recent implementation of new teacher certification requirements and teacher preparation program admissions requirements in the years from 1984 to 1989 resulted in a further decline in the numbers of teachers of color (Tillman, 2004). Other current events illustrate the continued maintenance of teaching as a white profession: following Hurricane Katrina, the entirety of a New Orleans school district's 7.500 employees, the vast majority of whom were Black, were fired, leading to devastating economic impacts on the surrounding community (Dixson, Buras, & Jeffers, 2015). The majority of these teachers and staff were replaced by white teachers. At this point, it is crucial to recognize that the historical legacy of teaching as a profession for "whites only" is still present in today's standards-based and outcomes-funded educational climate.

In conclusion, it is imperative that scholars, teacher educators, and policymakers recognize and take actions toward inclusion, recognizing that teachers and preservice teachers of color are still today excluded and marginalized within the teaching field. The historical legacy of the post-*Brown* ruling integration process and subsequent loss of teachers of color is often ignored in mainstream educational literature. Initiatives to recruit and retain teachers of color in the field must be informed by a sense of history of the United States' educational system, recognizing and understanding the reasons why teachers of color were historically pushed out of teaching and teacher certification programs in the first place. As long as the voices, experiences, and curricula of teachers of color are de-centered and ignored as integral to a high-quality educational system, inclusive of teachers of different backgrounds, whiteness will continue to play a crucial role in upholding its dominance over equitable and social just teaching.

Chapter 2

Colorblindness and the Need for Critical Whiteness Studies (CWS) in Education

ABSTRACT

Educational stakeholders, gatekeepers, and leaders who advocate for "equality" in public schools without also acknowledging white supremacy as the dominant ideology for the standards of pedagogy, curriculum, and assessment fail to account for how white privilege and white superiority are still maintained in today's educational system. Therefore, this chapter aims to detail the nuances of whiteness and deeply rooted racial prejudices that continue to marginalize teachers, students, and administrators of color, maintaining racialized social power imbalances (Hylton, 2005). The first section discusses the theoretical assumptions underpinning a Critical Whiteness Studies (CWS) perspective to problematize pedagogical racism embedded in mainstream school curricula. From this perspective, whiteness is a racial ideology yet also an invisible presence in schools that, in hidden ways, operates to "other" racialized identities when located in white educational spaces. The second section thus distinguishes the forms of invisibility whiteness takes on in order to maintain racialized power imbalances, including discourses of meritocracy, colorblindness, and white privilege. The chapter concludes showing how, upheld by whiteness, the teacher pipeline still today reproduces the racialization process, implicitly functioning to exclude and marginalize teachers, preservice teachers, and faculty of color. Given that the majority of teacher education programs are predominantly white, this means that many preservice teachers of color enter the profession against a backdrop of whiteness.

Social justice scholars have argued that whiteness and racism are still pervasive within the educational system in the United States (Gillborn, 2005;

Leonardo, 2009). Whiteness is upheld and validated, in part, through national and state policies functioning as "gatekeepers" in schooling. However, "gatekeeping" often works in hidden ways, thus sustaining white cultural practices, privilege, and pedagogies as dominant ideology and as difficult to name, reveal, and disrupt in learning contexts (Bonilla-Silva, 2006). In today's public schools, whiteness is centralized and revered through public processes such as formal de-segregation practices, legislature that dictates funding based on student performance, and the creation and support of charter and private academies. In explicit and implicit complex ways, the implementation of Eurocentric curricula and pedagogies, policymakers', teachers', and administrators' white values and backgrounds, along with white interest convergence—all together occupy an "othering" process that continues to marginalize community members of color in education, including students, teachers, staff, and administrators (Harper, Patton, & Wooden, 2009; Ladson-Billings, 2004). Teaching may now be considered a white profession, given that the population of teachers of color in the United States is less than 20 percent, despite a rapidly diversifying K-12 student population (NCES, 2018b). Notably, the number of teachers of color in the United States has barely increased over the past fifty years, and even decreased for some historically oppressed populations such as, for instance, Black teachers. In addition, the vast majority of key decision-makers regarding the educational content, funding, sourcing, and implementation (e.g., lawmakers, policymakers, stakeholders, and national task forces) have historically been and still are white (Bonilla-Silva, 2006).

While overt or explicit prejudice against teachers and students of color is less socially acceptable than it was prior to the *Brown vs Board of Education* ruling in 1954 and the civil rights movement, it is evident that in today's "colorblind" educational landscape, race still plays a crucial role in the current educational climate. This second chapter aims to examine how whiteness within the current climate of schooling continues to privilege racialized hierarchies, maintaining public education as an oppressive educational system for communities of color (Ladson-Billings & Tate, 1995). Addressing whiteness in the educational system exposes the insensitive tenor of educators, administrators, and policy/lawmakers who embrace a "raceless" approach to education, and sheds light on their refusal to examine how the processes of whiteness, in implicit ways, continue to marginalize teachers and students of color in schools, positioning them as "others."

Notions of colorblindness are often coded through safe or generic terms such as "multicultural education" or "diversity" in educational rhetoric. Through these codes, educators frequently take up discourses of colorblindness within schools, informed by a neoliberalist discourse that assumes any individual purportedly has an "equal" opportunity to succeed (Leonardo,

2007). Educational stakeholders, gatekeepers, and leaders who advocate for "equality" in schools without also acknowledging white supremacy as the dominant ideology for the standards of pedagogy, curriculum, and assessment fail to consider how white privilege and white superiority are still maintained in today's educational system. Therefore, this chapter aims to detail the nuances of whiteness deeply rooted in racial prejudices that continue to marginalize school community members of color in education, maintaining racialized social power imbalances (Hylton, 2005). First, the initial aim of this chapter is to discuss the theoretical assumptions underpinning a CWS perspective to problematize pedagogical racism in education. From this perspective, whiteness is a racial ideology yet also an invisible presence in schools that, in hidden ways, operates to "other" historically oppressed racialized identities when located in white spaces. Next, the second aim of this chapter is to highlight the forms of invisibility whiteness takes on in order to maintain racialized power imbalances, including discourses of meritocracy, colorblindness, and white privilege. Finally, the third aim is to utilize CWS to reveal and discuss the teacher pipeline as an example of how the racialization of schooling and subsequent exclusion take concrete forms in education. Given that the majority of teacher education programs are predominantly white, this means that many preservice teachers of color enter the profession against a backdrop of whiteness.

MAINTAINING WHITENESS AS THE INVISIBLE "NORM" IN PUBLIC SCHOOLS: A CWS PERSPECTIVE

The evidence of how whiteness is upheld and normalized within the educational system in the United States is first and foremost detailed in the demographic statistics of students, teachers, administrators, preservice teachers, graduate students, teacher education programs, and faculty in higher education. The significance of the make-up of the demographics of these populations *cannot* be overstated. Public school student demographics are rapidly shifting and over 50 percent of the students in the K-12 public school system in the United States now identify as students of color (NCES, 2017; U.S. Department of Education, 2016). In stark contrast, over 80 percent of the 3.2 million public school teachers and the 0.5 million private school teachers in the United States are white. School principals in both public and private schools represent similar demographic imbalances. In higher education, teacher education programs, graduate students and preservice teachers (teacher candidates) are 73 percent white (U.S. Department of Education, 2016). Faculty in degree-granting postsecondary institutions, including teacher preparation programs, are 76 percent white (NCES, 2017). Teachers of color are vastly overrepresented (42 percent) in schools that have both high percentages of students of color as well as high rates of poverty among the families. The trend of teachers of color concentrated in schools that serve predominantly students of color from low socioeconomic status households was first recognized in 1987 and has only increased since (NCES, 2017). Notably, there has been almost no growth in the number of teachers of color in low-poverty (i.e., white) schools, which employ only 15 percent of the entire teachers of color workforce (NCES, 2017). The broad disparity between the proportion of students of color populations within the United States (over 50 percent) in contrast with the overwhelming number of white educators from elementary school through graduate school (over 75 percent) clearly illustrates how whiteness is dominant within the teaching profession. These numbers indicate that whiteness is still central in its power-hold on gatekeeping, resource-distributing, and policymaking processes within education. These figures also represent a valid justification for the need to continue to critically examine, dissect, and disrupt whiteness within education as the dominant culture in order to facilitate educational success via authentic and meaningful experiences for teachers of color within a broad spectrum of school contexts.

An emerging branch of scholarship called CWS represents a shift away from focusing on the racialized experiences of students, teachers, and administrators of color to interrogate what it means to be white and to explore how whiteness is still pervasive in current institutions of schooling. This relatively recent field problematizes whiteness as a function of normative processes. While whiteness is invisible, taken for granted, or (un)intentionally centered and institutionalized in the United States educational system, CWS provides a critical approach useful in dismantling white supremacy, disrupting white normativity, and exposing whiteness as an "active system of domination" in schools (Levine-Rasky, 2000a, p. 264). Matias, Viesca, Garrison-Wade, Tandon, and Galindo (2014) write that the "normative script of white supremacy is an exertion of whiteness that refuses to acknowledge how whiteness is historically, economically, and legally produced" (p. 292). In other words, the act of turning away from the ways in which whiteness is cultivated and sustained as status quo affords white people a comfortable complacency with whiteness as "normal" while ignoring its "othering" and discriminatory practices. As an often intangible and unmentionable entity, the discourse of whiteness as the "natural order of things" can be seriously damaging in schools, and when unproblematized, can result in the dehumanization of students of color, along with a loss of agency, while protecting "greater material advantages . . . through white territorial practices" (Allen, 2014, p. 124).

CWS rejects the notion of fixed whiteness as a phenomenon, given the social construction and fluidity of race (Arnesen, 2001). While whiteness is salient in relation to racialized exploitation and injustice in the history of the

United States, it is crucial to avoid resorting to broad overgeneralizations or losing the specific context within which whiteness is located and institutionalized (Kolchin, 2002). It can be easy to mistakenly conflate race, nationality, and ethnicity but these nuances should be interrogated from a sociocultural paradigm, in contextual terms, when engaging in critical work on whiteness and racial inequity or inequality. The concept of whiteness in this case extends beyond physical features and institutions; whiteness instead refers to the "unthinking assumptions and actions" that most white teachers embody and, consciously or unconsciously, perform in their daily lives (Gillborn, 2005, p. 486). However, whiteness is also socially constructed, taken for granted as normal, and difficult to pinpoint because of its elevated position as natural or invisible. Moreover, the use of the term "whiteness" does not refer to the acts of an individual white person; rather, it refers to a systematic infrastructure that "bestows unearned power and privilege onto those who approximate as white" (Allen, 2014, p. 130).

Whiteness and race have long been established as fluid constructs within social science fields, including education. CWS as a discipline focuses on the idea that whiteness is a racial ideology, functioning much like other racial ideologies except that it is often normalized and institutionalized to the point of invisibility (Allen, 2014; Levine-Rasky, 2006). In other words, while white principals and administrators in schools might identify teachers of color as having a "race" and often seek to classify and define teachers of color by their racialized identities, too often the descriptions of white teachers' racial identities remain either "unmarked" or are constructed as "normal" or "universal." CWS aims to dismiss this normalizing and racialized dichotomizing that maintains whiteness as viewed only in opposition to "other" races (Matias, 2013a). When whiteness is defined as a biological category and racially categorized as a binary, "race" is thus assembled in white terms, constructed and defined as normative in opposition to what it is not (i.e., "other" or "different") and positioned as the ruler in a racial hierarchy.

To destabilize whiteness and disrupt racial hierarchy, CWS advocates for an exploration of whiteness as racial ideology versus a biological determination, calling for an understanding of race as constructed in a specific historical Western moment. When whiteness holds power regarding political processes, law-making, and economic forces (Godfrey, 2008; Kolchin, 2002), white individuals positioned as stakeholders might (un)intentionally determine which historically marginalized groups are classified as white in opposition to "other" racially minoritized identities; in other words, whites determine who is considered "white." This social fluidity of whiteness has always been a crucial underpinning of legal doctrine and racialized hierarchies in the United States. For example, in 1848, the Treaty of Guadalupe Hidalgo guaranteed United Sstates citizenship to all "free white persons" in an attempt to exclude Black and Asian and Pacific Islander populations from this benefit, but this meant that Mexican Americans fell into the category considered as white (Godfrey, 2008). However, while Mexican Americans may have been legally classified as white, the majority of this population experienced social prejudice and racism unless they were light-skinned enough to "pass" as white. In another example, during the eighteenth and nineteenth centuries, Irish immigrant workers faced extreme prejudice on par with communities of color, and therefore put forth a concentrated effort to align themselves with whiteness and maintain racial hierarchies of dominance by defining themselves as free-willed and "American" in contrast to, for example, Black slaves (Arnesen, 2001; Kolchin, 2002). Additionally, anti-Semitic discourses have historically resulted in Jewish people being excluded from the category of "white" throughout United States and European history (Brodkin, 2002). These intersections of race, whiteness, and ethnicity shed light on how power differentials are constructed and furthered within economic systems, cultural interactions, and social processes to maintain whiteness as the status quo and at the top of a racialized hierarchical order (Levine-Rasky, 2016). Thus, it is clear from United States history that racial ideologies are not biologically determined but rather socially produced; a function of how economic, political, and sociocultural discourses produce race in a specific historical contingency.

The need to interrogate whiteness stems from the idea that whiteness is an "invisible marker [that] depends on the racial 'other' for its own identity" (Leonardo, 2004, p. 137). Whiteness thus defines individuals who are "absent color, absent of that which might make [one] other than white" and juxtaposes them against those who are "not white" (Hytten & Warren, 2003, p. 66). The naturalization of whiteness is produced and sustained by white supremacy as a sociocultural system functioning to "individually and collectively silence and subvert the counternarratives of people of color" (Allen, 2014, p. 125). The historical backdrop of white supremacy as policy within the United States serves as the foundation upon which systems of government, economic, educational, and law were built, and thus, controlled access to political, cultural, and economic capital for teachers, students, and communities. Over time, for historically oppressed groups, the lack of access and opportunities to equitable and well-funded schooling has produced the current "academic gap" (Yosso, 2005). To critically address today's "academic gap" between white and traditionally oppressed groups, there is an urgent need to integrate a CWS perspective into school curricula and practices.

CWS Pedagogies in School

Identifying and disrupting whiteness as a widespread notion in schools is a difficult endeavor because of its omnipresence yet simultaneous invisibility in social discourse. Leonardo (2009) describes whiteness in schools as "nowhere since it is unmarked and everywhere since it is the standard whereby other groups are judged" (p. 263). Drawing from a CWS perspective as a counter-hegemonic approach to addressing racism in education, social justice scholars have advocated for moving the focus of race issues beyond the "other"—for example, the identities and experiences of teachers of color—to critique the construction of whiteness as a normative notion (Kolchin, 2002). Scholars in education have employed CWS to disrupt the normalization or idolization of whiteness by naming whiteness, interrogating how whiteness as racial ideology has informed the school experiences of students, teachers, and administrators of color, revealing how white students, teachers, and administrators conceptualize, understand, and deal with race issues, and problematizing their complicit roles in white supremacy (Matias & Mackey, 2016).

Using CWS as a lens for examining racial inequity within school contexts can be beneficial to shed light on how whiteness operates in schools, thus helping educators identify, name, and destabilize the invisibility of whiteness, and learn how to implement antiracist and socially just pedagogies and curricula. For instance, Matias and Liou (2015) used CWS to engage in critical race teacher activism in a classroom with a high number of students of color and attempted to highlight and disrupt whiteness by implementing critical whiteness pedagogies. These pedagogies included rejecting Eurocentric curricula (e.g., "world history") for a multinational critique of colonialism and hegemonic whiteness, engaging in a "metacognition" of the meanings and relevancy of race within students' lives, and providing students with the vocabulary (e.g., "racial aggressions," "white supremacy") to assist them in critically making sense of and expressing their experiences of racialized injustice and prejudice. Informed by CWS, this pedagogical example illustrated how teachers' engagement in critical and transformative pedagogies *with* students of color has the potential to disrupt hegemonies of whiteness embedded within educational processes.

CWS can also be applied to pedagogy in classroom settings with white students to help them learn how to critically analyze and conceptualize their own understandings of race, and thus learn how to invest in becoming more critically aware and critically conscious about issues of race, injustice, and whiteness. Rogers and Mosley (2006) utilized critical literacy pedagogies framed by CWS to facilitate white second-graders' meaning-making, analysis, and critique of whiteness, and to construct a learning environment where both the students and the teacher became racially literate by learning how to identify whiteness and white privilege in their lives. Drawing from relevant literature, it can be suggested that critical pedagogies constructed and implemented from a CWS perspective have the potential to "make visible" the "hidden curriculum" of whiteness that implicitly aims to maintain dominance

within educational settings, creating a more socially just school context for
both students, teachers, and their communities.

WHITE SUPREMACY, THE INVISIBILITY/ HYPERVISIBILITY OF TEACHERS OF COLOR, AND THE PARADOX OF WHITENESS

White supremacy is "endemic and ingrained" within American society to
the point where "invisible racism" is considered normal or is even legislated
yet denied as racist (Boutte & Jackson, 2014, p. 625). In today's American
public schools, social spaces and interactions are often implicitly coded as
environments that "perpetuate white power and privilege while also making
it look like it is not happening" (Allen, 2014, p. 126). This "invisible racism"
is embedded into the structural blueprints of infrastructures such as schools
and universities, and normalized to a point of unrecognizability (Boutte &
Jackson, 2014). Yet, as Gillborn (2005) wrote, "one of the most powerful
and dangerous aspects of whiteness is that many . . . people have no awareness of whiteness" (p. 9). While notions of white supremacy and whiteness
are typically associated with outward acts of overt racism, this is misleading:
whiteness signifies how white power and dominance, in complex and hidden
ways, uphold political, economic, and sociocultural systems, including the
educational institution of schooling (Gillborn, 2006). The notion of whiteness
is not open, tangible, and easily identifiable. In other words, whiteness is not
typically characterized by overt racist incidents such as a white supremacist
group rally, a "Whites Only" sign at a restaurant, or a noose hanging outside
a Black student's locker (Howard-Woods, Laidley, & Omidi, 2018). Rather,
whiteness is enacted in implicit ways via an utter dominance of whiteness
that functions to center white experiences, identities, and feelings while
simultaneously "othering" the experiences, identities, and feelings of people
of color. Thus, structural whiteness works as an invisible form of racism that
produces a racialized binary of white versus "nonwhite" in the United States.
This racialized binary reinforces whiteness and at the same time, polices the
actions, attitudes, and identities of teachers of color, positioning them as
"outsiders" in schools.

Its invisibility is what makes whiteness so influential in American society,
and what makes white privilege "powerful yet power-evasive" (Haviland,
2008, p. 44). To be white often means to attain some modicum of power.
However, most whites would deny or ignore that they hold this power,
and this denial reproduces an invisible or unacknowledged cycle of white
dominance. For example, the case of white teachers' and administrators'
positioning of teachers of color as "different," "other," or "ineffective" in

predominantly white schools is an example of whites' denial of holding onto and using their power, in implicit ways, over teachers of color, along with the racialization of teaching. When whites deny that they hold and use power over "others," who are defined as "different" in opposition to "whites," then the ideologies of whiteness and inherent imbalanced power dynamics are rarely, if ever, troubled or problematized. Teachers of color who work in predominantly white schools are often forced into a racialized position from which they have to consistently navigate imbalanced power dynamics of whiteness, negotiating, making sense, and struggling against the minoritization of their experiences and identities.

Within broad systems and institutions of the United States lie the invisibility of whiteness, carefully coded in neutral language that prevents any challenges to the institutionalization of racial hierarchy. In the current educational system, for example, whiteness as the dominant culture in many schools works to police teachers of color's identities, "racializing" and "otherizing" their identities in negative terms. This policing limits their ability to "trickle into white spaces," (Leonardo, 2009, p. 98), thus safeguarding the centered position white teachers occupy and upholding the unequal distributions of power inscribed by whiteness and institutionalized in schools.

Within these institutions, the invisibility of whiteness often manifests itself as discourses of meritocracy, colorblindness, and white privilege. A meritocratic approach, or the idea that rewards and success are bestowed upon those who most deserve them, serves to reinforce white domination and subsequent subordination of teachers of color by turning an "innocent" gaze toward racialized individuals in white terms. This approach dismisses the historical legacy of white supremacy and the importance of access for historically oppressed groups to the educational, sociocultural, and economic capital needed to advance in society. As a result of using a meritocratic approach, race-based inequity is often overlooked and replaced with a colorblind individualist approach that positions teachers of color as "failures" because they are unable to reach similar achievements to those of their white teacher counterparts (Leonardo, 2009). Further, many whites' adoption of a meritocractic approach is often utilized to protect opportunities and access to sociocultural, political, and economic resources, maintaining white privilege on the one hand, and on the other hand, preventing teachers of color from having opportunities to access the cultural and economic capital necessary for academic progress. In a meritocractic approach, when positioned as "other" teachers, teachers of color are constructed as responsible for their own failures. As such, they are then blamed for their "failings," and the cultural knowledges and pedagogical approaches to teaching by teachers of color are devalued.

In addition to meritocratic discourses, notions of colorblindness are common within the United States, particularly in educational contexts. According to Leonardo (2009), a colorblind perspective supports the idea that acts of racism are declining, isolated, and occur at a singular or individual level, while simultaneously problematizing teachers of color as responsible for their own failures by discourse that dismisses, ignores, and refuses to "see" race. Colorblindness within educational contexts grants permission for white teachers, policymakers, stakeholders, gatekeepers, and administrators to disregard the link between history, academic achievement, and the racial organization of society, positioning all teachers and students as "equals" (Leonardo, 2009). Rather than acknowledging the systematic, structural, and historical implications of slavery, prejudice, and racism, manifestations of white supremacy are overlooked or denied, and individualistic meritocratic discourses or singular instances of racial "progress" are celebrated and heralded as markers of a "neutral" or an "even" playing field. By ignoring the identities and cultural capital of entire marginalized groups who are culturally distant from the expectations or demands of a white-driven educational culture, colorblind curricula and pedagogies continue to be enacted in school contexts with little to no problematization. The legitimization of a colorblind perspective, or the circulation of a "raceless" approach, allows white teachers and administrators in schools to avoid their own discomfort with discussing race and racial inequality, thus failing to engage with and problematize white privilege or address racialized pedagogies and curricula (Boutte & Jackson, 2014, p. 626).

Another form of whiteness that operates in invisible ways but takes concrete form in schooling is how white privilege and white tears are prioritized over the experiences, identities, and emotions of teachers of color. These manifestations of whiteness prevent the racial advancement of a social justice agenda in schools through the consistent validation of the emotional discomfort and pain of white teachers or administrators feel when they are invited and challenged to engage and deal with the notion of white privilege and white supremacy. White tears create, in material ways, racialized spaces where the emotions and pain of teachers of color are secondary to white emotions (Leonardo, 2002; Matias, 2016). Discourses of whiteness as "normal" legitimate, validate, and prioritize white teachers' and administrators' emotional discomfort with topics around whiteness and racism, shifting the focus from addressing the issues of race at hand to ensuring any upset white teacher or administrator are relieved from the possibilities of being seen as "racist," "biased," or "unfair." White performativity of emotional discomfort and emotional need for reassurance serves, intentionally or unintentionally, to reaffirm white privilege and reifies whiteness as prioritized and revered (Matias, 2016). As white tears are validated and used to gain sympathy when expressing remorse, guilt, or discomfort over racist incidents, or opinions, white teachers and administrators can continue to legitimate their position as victims, ignoring, undermining, or putting aside the emotions, values, and experiences of teachers of color. This white performance centers whiteness through negative emotions and claims the sympathies of other whites nearby (Leonardo, 2002). The paradox of whiteness as both invisible yet ubiquitous means that white privilege, through the emotional expression of white pain and white tears, is normalized, and thus elevated over the pain of teachers of color's emotions, experiences, and struggles against racism on a daily basis.

When whiteness is normalized, rendered invisible, taken for granted, and idealized, then any "other" identity positioned against a backdrop of whiteness can be constructed as oppositional to these descriptions: abnormal, highly visible, "inappropriate," "unusual," and less-than-ideal. In this way, as Allen (2014) stated, the "definition of 'humanity' takes on a white face, a white gait, a white sound, and a white mentality. 'White,' 'normal,' and 'human' converge into a disturbing synonymous relationship" (p. 126). As such, teachers of color, simply by their virtue of being "nonwhite," become hypervisible—overtly visible as nonwhite—negative representations of a "normative identity" within predominantly white school contexts. Teachers of color who enter traditionally white spaces, such as schools or institutions of higher education, are, as minoritized members of the community, instantly singled out and made hypervisible simply by their physical self-representation existing within a sea of whiteness. Teachers of color in white spaces cannot "blend in" and therefore are forced to conform to whiteness in these spaces, attempting to live up to white expectations and standards while teaching within a dominant culture of whiteness that does not acknowledge, legitimate, and validate who they are. Ultimately, the emotional load of hypervisibility by being marked by race in predominantly white educational spaces takes its toll on many teachers of color, frequently resulting in long-term anxiety, emotional struggle, and identity turmoil (Matias, 2013a).

Through notions of meritocracy, colorblindness, and white privilege, white tears, and white pain, whiteness protects its status quo symbol as the "American way." Thus, any "other" individual who identifies outside the center of whiteness is inherently marginalized as "different," and therefore denied access to social, cultural, and economic capital produced and maintained by white privilege. Through the lenses of the "American way," the implications for teachers of color, particularly those located within predominantly white schools, are the consistent, implicit or explicit, racialized marks that position them as outsiders or "othered" within a teaching profession dominated by whiteness. Being forced to continuously negotiate whiteness and a "marked" or racialized identity can lead to significant emotional and identity duress for teachers of color.

CWS AND TEACHER EDUCATION PROGRAMS

CWS as a framework can be particularly valuable for teacher education programs to critically examine the notions of white supremacy—from Eurocentric curricula, national and state standards of teacher competency based on white norms and ideals, to programs that do not value or prioritize culturally relevant and antiracist pedagogies. Teacher education programs are often "tied up in the production, valuation, and distribution of structural or scientific knowledge in ways that privilege whiteness" (Allen, 2014, p. 131). Examining teacher education research from a CWS perspective provides a prime example of how whiteness functions as an invisible controller while, at the same time and especially in predominantly white spaces, creates a climate of hypervisibility for community members of color (e.g., teacher education programs, teacher educators, and preservice teachers).

In order to understand how teachers are socialized into the profession within a culture of whiteness, and given the vast preponderance of white teachers within our educational system, it is imperative to examine the teacher pipeline, or the system in which new teachers are "produced." The teacher pipeline reproduces racialized power differentials, reinforcing on the one hand white hegemonies both within individual classroom settings and across schools, districts, states, and at the national level, and on the other hand, promoting a "white savior" role for white teacher candidates who desire to teach in urban schools serving predominantly communities of color (Matias & Liou, 2015; Matias & Mackey, 2016). In other words, how preservice teachers learn the processes of teaching within their teacher education programs is often, implicitly, coded in white, middle-class norms. Teachers and students of color, along with schools serving communities of color, are frequently positioned as "less than" these educational standards; thus, they are constructed in need of "help" or in need of being "saved" by white preservice teachers (Matias, 2013a).

Even when teacher education programs serve a significant population of preservice teachers of color, the preservice teachers still have to pass state-mandated certification requirements. These requirements, such as high-stakes teacher certification testing or student-teaching scenarios, often place little value on knowledge and pedagogies that are not white-centered. An analysis of the state teaching licensure exam in California revealed minimal content knowledge in social studies about racial history in the United States, showing a Eurocentric approach that validates a "white-only" perspective on history and curricula (Perez Huber, Johnson, & Kohli, 2006). There is a significant gap between white preservice teachers and preservice teachers of color on the pass rate of state licensure exams, and moreover, researchers determined that white students' success in these exams is often at the expense of students of color's success (Goldhaber & Hansen, 2010; Nettles, Scatton, Steinberg, & Tyler, 2011). For example, the Praxis exams used for teacher licensure testing in forty-one states are appropriate predictors to demonstrate teacher readiness and quality for white female students but not for students of color (Petchauer, 2012). At the same time, the Praxis teacher certification exams have empirical gaps in passing rates that are distributed across racial demographics and strongly suggested to be culturally biased against preservice teachers of color (Bennett, McWhorter, & Kuykendall, 2006; Grant, 2004). Stereotype threats, or the internalized feelings of fear and anxiety over being viewed through a racialized lens, has also been demonstrated to be a significantly detrimental factor in the exam performances and pass rates by students of color, particularly in high-stakes testing such as teacher certification exams (Steele, 2011). Thus, gatekeeping processes in teacher education such as certification tests demonstrate how whiteness is invisibly embedded, resulting in a notable barrier for preservice teachers of color to gain access to employment and a future in the profession.

Teacher education programs socialize new teachers into the profession as the primary channel in the teacher pipeline, providing a wheelhouse of tools, pedagogies, and socio-educational resources for teacher candidates to explore their identity, cultural background, experiences, and aspirations to become teachers. But as the majority of these teacher candidates are white, and almost 80 percent of teacher educators (e.g., institution faculty members) are white, whiteness rarely gets checked, disrupted, or culturally problematized within these programs (Milner, Pearman & McGee, 2013). The whiteness of teacher education faculty is a huge factor in determining what is included in preservice teacher curricula, how new students and new faculty are recruited, selected, and retained within programs, and how issues of racial inequality and diversity are addressed as part of faculty's curricula and teaching (Sleeter, 2017). "Diversity work" is often separated out within teacher education programs through the form of a single "multicultural education" course while the rest of the teacher education curriculum sequence gives minimal, if any, attention to issues of diversity, whiteness, and inequity (King & Butler, 2015). This "bracketing" of diversity work means that teacher education programs are limited in how they prepare students for teaching in schools with high numbers of students of color (Sleeter, 2017). For instance, Matias et al. (2014) argued that teacher beliefs play a large role in maintaining whiteness within schools yet teacher education programs do little to try to encourage white teacher candidates to reflect on their whiteness and white privilege. To explore this idea further, Matias and Mackey (2016) utilized CWS to examine how white teacher candidates experienced emotions of whiteness, such as guilt, anger, and defensiveness, while also determining if and how self-reflective pedagogies facilitated white teacher candidates' reflections on

denial, colorblindness, and deflection, along with the development of critical awareness, consciousness, and pedagogical growth. Given the processes
of the professional phase of teacher socialization through teacher education
programs and the significant lack of teachers of color within increasingly
diverse yet de facto segregated public school contexts, acknowledging how
the teacher pipeline, through majority white teacher certification programs,
reinforces and legitimates whiteness and white supremacy within schools is
particularly relevant (Amos, 2016; Sleeter, 2017; Tatum, 2017).

In this vein, researchers have pointed out that even when teacher educators
aim to adopt culturally relevant or antiracist pedagogies within their courses
or teacher certification programs, white preservice teachers effectively resist
disrupting discourses of whiteness as a means of "actively protect[ing] their
hegemonic stories and white supremacy" (Boutte & Jackson, 2014, p. 627).
For example, white teacher candidates and teacher educators have been found
to be supremely invested in their whiteness, refusing to engage with notions
of race and racism, thus taking up a colorblind perspective that continues
the cycle of white supremacy within educational contexts (Matias et al.,
2014; Levine-Rasky, 2000a,b). Further, when teacher education faculty *do*
address issues of racialized power and oppression within teaching contexts,
white preservice teachers may be more likely to give these faculty negative
teaching evaluation scores. This pedagogical stance then becomes a serious
risk for faculty members' tenure track position, tenure process, and performance evaluation (Evans-Winters & Hoff, 2011). Those risks are even more
problematic for teacher education faculty of color in tenure track positions,
since they already face racialized bias regarding student evaluations of their
teaching and courses. Notions of whiteness and racism are often disregarded,
avoided, or "glossed over" by white teacher candidates in favor of safer, de-
racialized approaches coded in the language of "diversity," "multiculturalism," and "sameness" (Haviland, 2008). This denial reinforces and preserves
the status quo—white privilege—using colorblind pedagogies that do not
address unequal power relations but rather reinstate whiteness and its coded
terms (Amos, 2016; Levine-Rasky, 2000b). Through resistance, denial, and
even anger at the idea of race, white teacher educators and preservice teachers normalize their white experiences and viewpoints and deny that whiteness
has an impact on what they see as "just," "true," or "real" (Bonilla-Silva &
Embrick, 2006; Matias, 2013a).

In contrast to the experiences of white teacher candidates, who hold onto
their white privilege, rarely having to acknowledge or think about race,
racism, and racial inequality, preservice teachers of color are left having
to negotiate hypervisibility—daily reminders of their racialized identities
as "nonwhite" or as "other," along with exclusion and marginalization,
(Brunsma, Embrick, & Shin, 2017; Solórzano, 1998). Teachers of color

frequently become teacher-certified in predominantly white teacher educa-tion programs, and thus are a part of and participate in a pipeline of teacher "production" informed by whiteness (NCES, 2018a; Solórzano & Bernal, 2001). Both teacher candidates of color who desire to work in schools serving communities of color in an effort to give back, as well as those who pursue teaching careers in predominantly white schools, are frequently confronted with dominant ideologies of whiteness. In the first case, as they transition to full-time teachers in the field, teachers of color might end up teaching in diverse school districts, where funding allocations are limited and/or based on student performances on state or national standards of assessment that are culturally biased or grounded in whiteness. In the second case, for teachers of color who teach in schools with a predominantly white population, white-ness as ideology is pervasive, making racial confrontations often inevitable yet invisible for teachers of color. Further, the majority of teacher candidates of color attend "traditional" four-year institutions mostly in suburban or rural locations. In general, this means that many preservice teachers of color are socialized into teaching at white schools, from pre-practicum work to student teaching to the curricula and pedagogies normalized as "acceptable" within their predominantly white teacher institutions (Sleeter, 2017). Thus, for many preservice teachers of color, ideologies of whiteness ubiquitously shape their cultural knowledge and educational capital as "different" from the "norm," disavowing or ignoring their experiences of isolation or marginalization at predominantly white institutions (Kohli & Pizarro, 2016).

Notably, preservice teachers of color experience higher rates of racial aggressions, prejudice, stereotyping, and discrimination than their white counterparts, as well as an overall uncomfortable or "chilly" climate within their teacher education programs, and are negatively impacted by their white counterparts' colorblind or race-resistant behaviors (Amos, 2016; Berry, 2005; Sleeter, 2001; Yosso, Smith, Ceja, & Solórzano, 2009). The predomi-nance of white faculty in teacher education programs means that preservice teachers of color often feel their professors do not understand or "see" the need for culturally relevant teaching within schools serving communities of color. White faculty at teacher education programs also are perceived by preservice teachers of color as not being open or receptive to ideas beyond traditional white conceptions of teaching (Irizarry, 2011). Additionally, pre-service teachers of color often feel like they need to "blend in" within pre-dominantly white campuses and teacher education programs in spite of the forced visibility of their physical self-representations as they may be "singled out" as an "expert" in diversity (Gomez, Rodriguez, & Agosto, 2008; Lewis, Chesler, & Forman, 2000).

Current research on the experiences of teacher candidates of color indicates a higher dropout rate compared to their white counterparts. This means that students are not well supported and find themselves excluded as members of their educational community while simultaneously managing increased negative emotions and anxiety in a cultural context that does not validate their identities and cultural knowledge (Amos, 2016; Brunsma et al., 2017; Yosso et al., 2009). Thus, given the structural barriers that protect and maintain whiteness as well as the additional psychological and emotional burden of a racialized identity in a sea of whiteness, it can be difficult for preservice teachers of color to feel legitimated, acknowledged, and achieve professional success in teacher education programs.

When preservice teachers of color are consistently reminded that their cultural knowledge is less-worthy than that of their white counterparts, they may internalize this view to the point where they are unable to recognize their own cultural contributions to educational contexts (Kohli, 2008). Many teachers of color have been educated by an "oppressive schooling system that promotes white cultural values . . . and [are] socialized to see nonwhite cultural knowledge as inferior to that of the dominant culture" (Kohli, 2014, p. 372). Therefore, it is important that teacher education programs provide time and space for preservice teachers to reflect on how their racialized knowledge and experiences have impacted their values, attitudes, or worldviews. This is true for both white teacher candidates, who may never have come to terms with the notion of white privilege; and/or for teacher candidates of color, who may have been indoctrinated by white supremacy into de-valuing the set of cultural wisdom and knowledges they bring to a classroom, and perhaps have never been provided with a chance to name this indoctrination as a form of racialized education (Kohli, 2008).

Education in the United States has long-standing historical connections to Eurocentric curricula and pedagogy that prioritize and center whiteness and white community members while marginalizing the "other," or those who fall outside the borders of the accepted norms of teaching and learning (Gay, 2010; Ladson-Billings, 2001; Tatum, 2017). In teacher education, faculty and preservice teachers alike need to unlearn the codes of whiteness which translate to white privilege, white dominance, white normalization, and a clear racial hierarchy which polices and marginalizes racialized identities (Leonardo, 2009). The teacher pipeline consistently delivers a minute number of teachers who are capable of both competently supporting students of color and who are able to effectively or willingly address racism within educational contexts (Sleeter, 2016). It is evident that a new framework for teacher education is necessary, one informed by a socio-critical perspective that can guide preservice teachers in problematizing and confronting racial inequity and inequality within their classrooms; encourage preservice teachers to develop social justice pedagogies to facilitate student development of a critical consciousness and understandings of race relations; and promote white preservice teacher reflection, creating dialogue centered around the notions of whiteness, white privilege, and white supremacy.

CONCLUSION

This chapter discusses how whiteness is normalized and institutionalized within educational ecologies through discourses of meritocracy, colorblindness, and white privilege, resulting in a hypervisibility of teachers of color in white spaces. Current research on the topic has identified myriad ways in which a white hegemony is preserved at the expense of both the educational success and the emotional or psychological well-being of teachers of color, especially when they teach in predominantly white school contexts (Kohli, 2008; Lewis et al., 2000; Matias, 2016). Regarding the teacher pipeline, the ideology of whiteness is so pervasive in the United States that it is often unrecognized or invisible yet extraordinarily powerful in maintaining a racial hierarchy that implicitly positions white preservice teachers and teacher education faculty in a dominant, normative position and teachers of color as "other," or subordinate. Within the context of teacher education programs, the invisibility of whiteness means that many white preservice teachers and faculty are unable to identify whiteness as a force in shaping their understanding of race relations in schools and their own racialized identities. However, whiteness as "normal" continues to be pervasive within educational contexts, creating a sense of hypervisibility for teachers and preservice teachers of color, and reinforcing a deficit approach in schools and teacher education programs with high concentrations of teachers, students, and administrators of color.

Alternatively, in predominantly white teacher training programs and schools where whiteness is enacted daily, the examples provided in this chapter shed light on how white supremacy is circulated, reproduced, and reinforced by both student and faculty populations, consciously or unconsciously, because they often lack critical pedagogical tools to identify or address the invisible, normative paradigm of whiteness. However, because of their key role in the teacher socialization process and the teacher pipeline, social justice scholars have advocated for the need to reframe and integrate a social justice agenda into teacher education programs to provide learning environments that promote critical awareness, critical consciousness, and critical understanding of race, whiteness, and education. There is an urgent need for teacher education programs first to reject a generic "multicultural" approach in favor of one that interrogates race-based injustice. Second, teacher education programs must provide a curriculum that critically examines and deconstructs invisible whiteness to intentionally reveal, address, and dismiss racist teacher views, beliefs, and attitudes (e.g., "white savior complex"). Finally, moving beyond the "single course" approach to "multiculturalism," teacher education programs need to reconceptualize the curriculum to embed critical race and critical whiteness pedagogies across the sequence of their teacher certification courses. While research indicates that growth in critical approaches to race and racism is possible within teacher education programs committed to a social justice agenda, promoting and centering antiracist pedagogies in order to better prepare white teachers for working in schools that serve communities of color needs to happen on a broader scale (Sleeter, 2017). Given the significant cultural disconnect between the majority white teacher and teacher educator populations and the rapidly diversifying student population, it is clear that whiteness will remain dominant and prioritized within education and classrooms until teacher education programs intentionally commit to antiracist and social justice pedagogies.

Chapter 3

Critical Race Theory to Develop a Critical Consciousness

Understanding "Racism as Structure"

ABSTRACT

Racism as structure is a useful notion to understand how teachers of color positioned as "other" teachers in predominantly white schools become subordinated "beneath" their white teacher or preservice teacher counterparts. The first section of the chapter builds upon the social construction of the term "racism" within the United States to explore Bonilla-Silva's (2006) conceptualization of "racism as structure." The second section of the chapter shows how racism as structure takes shape within schools via white teachers and administrators' actions, attitudes, and beliefs in a multitude of ways, including taking up the notion of "reverse racism" to preserve white privilege and power. Maintaining white privilege is then further problematized using white interest convergence theory to interrogate how social justice gains within education might be incurred only when whites in power either perceive personal benefits to these gains or a minimal loss of access to resources and socio-educational, political, and economic capital. To challenge whiteness, the chapter concludes by discussing the assumptions underpinning critical race theory (CRT) and intersectionality to provide a useful framework for exploring, understanding, and centering the storytelling by teachers of color of their teaching experiences in predominantly white school contexts.

The previous chapters discuss how the historical legacy of white supremacy within schools and educational policy is still pervasive, and the complex ways in which whiteness functions as an ideology in today's educational ecologies. The current critical approach toward the centering of whiteness in education strongholds a convincing argument for the need for wider and more authentic engagement with culturally relevant and sustaining pedagogies. In doing so, teachers and preservice teachers can develop a critical consciousness regarding racism and racialized inequity as structural or systemic across social strata within the United States. One of the goals of better understanding CRT as an ontological perspective is to help educators interrogate issues of race, racism, and whiteness, thus raising critical consciousness in the classroom to foster a social justice agenda. It is therefore vital that teachers, teacher educators, and scholars in education have opportunities to grapple with and conceptualize what the term "racism" means in the current colorblind era, and what "racism as structure" looks like in the United States.

Drawing from Bonilla-Silva's work (2006, 2015) on the notion of "racism as structure," this chapter aims to problematize the overlying imbalanced power dynamics that function to sustain pedagogical "otherness" and "normativity" in the educational landscape, providing a lens from which the structures of racism embedded within educational contexts are critically examined (Jennings & Lynn, 2005). Therefore, the first section of the chapter discusses the social construction of the term "racism" within the United States, and explores Bonilla-Silva's (2006) conceptualization of "racism as structure." In particular, this section demonstrates how dominant discourses of colorblindness, meritocracy, and white universality are utilized to maintain "racism as structure" within educational contexts by normalizing whiteness, thus making inherent racism hard to see, name, or destabilize. The second section of the chapter shows how racism as structure takes shape within schools via white teachers and administrators' actions, attitudes, and beliefs in a multitude of ways, including taking up, consciously or unconsciously, the notion of "reverse racism" to preserve white privilege and power. The third section of the chapter uses white interest convergence theory to problematize how social justice gains within education might be incurred when whites in power either perceive personal benefits to these gains or a minimal loss of access to resources and socio-educational, political, and economic capital. The final section of the chapter discusses the assumptions underpinning CRT and intersectionality, using the main tenets of CRT in order to provide a framework for exploring, understanding, and centering teachers of color's storytelling of their work in predominantly white school contexts.

FROM THE JIM CROW ERA TO "RACISM AS STRUCTURE" IN COLORBLIND TIMES

Most Americans are familiar with the term racism. However, critical race scholars have challenged the assumptions underpinning this notion, arguing that the notion of "racism" in today's colorblind times is more than the basic act of negatively judging or disliking someone based on the color of their skin (Bonilla-Silva, 2006; Lopez, 2003; Milner, 2013; Parker, 2019). The conventional or naive conceptualization of racism as skin-based is problematic for multiple reasons. First, this approach presents an individualistic and simplistic perspective on racism, lacks historical context, and does not take into account the systematic or structural means through which race, racism, and colorblindness are institutionalized in the social fabric of the United States. Second, the historical legacies of indigenous colonization, African enslavement, the exploitation of racialized labor for white profit, legalized discrimination against Black, Indigenous, and people of color, and legislated policies all frame an understanding of racism that extends far beyond a person-to-person negative interaction dependent upon racial identities. Instead, "racism as structure" recognizes racism as an ideology that has taken concrete form over time as a result of the historical domination of whiteness in society (Bonilla-Silva, 2015).

Specifically, Bonilla-Silva (2015) described racism as the "practices and behaviors that produce a racial structure—a network of social relations at social, political, and economic levels that shape the life chances of the various races" (p. 1360). In other words, racism takes place, often in veiled ways, through powerful racialized ideologies that circulate in society as well as through foundational racialized structures such as laws, policies, and unquestioned beliefs automatically assumed to be true. Although race is acknowledged as fluid, and intangible, it is also the structure that produces systematic institutionalized inequality for some while elevating others through a host of advantages that privilege dominant groups. While social justice scholars have often depicted race as a socially constructed notion, however, when racialized ideologies take structural forms in institutions such as schooling, long-term ramifications of racial inequalities become severe and difficult to address. Expanding on the notion of race as a socially constructed concept to race as an ideology that has "material and consequential" (Bonilla-Silva, 2015, p. 1361) impacts on identities, the term racism bears multiple, complicated social meanings that, in overt or covert ways, maintain claims of colorblindness, meritocracy, white universality, and white interest convergence as structural in society (Bonilla-Silva, 2015).

Colorblindness and Meritocracy

Dominant narratives of colorblindness in the United States currently sustain the idea that the majority of Americans would give lip service to condemning open or overt racism. Additional tropes within this narrative include the condemnation of discrimination regarding access to public services based on skin color, and that "racism" was a part of the United States' past but does not play a significant role in today's American society. However, social justice scholars have written extensively on the complex ways in which structural racism is still in place and institutionalized in the United States but often ignored or rendered invisible, thus making it challenging to be "seen" by white eyes. As more time passes from the civil rights movement, meaning less Americans remember the movement, in today's increasingly neoliberal globalized society, the United States' current approach to race is framed by positions of colorblindness and meritocracy that aim to obscure social inequalities and silence, rather than voice and name, race and racial inequity (Leonardo, 2007). For instance, many white educators' resistance to acknowledging the centrality of race (or lack thereof) in current public school curricula continues to produce a cycle of ignoring, dismissing, or disavowing race-based difference, racial discrimination, and exclusion (Leonardo, 2007). This colorblind discourse takes up the position that race does not matter any longer in education, refusing to account for racial disparities that are still institutionalized in today's legal doctrine and social or structural policies.

As Bonilla-Silva's (2006) work illustrates, a conceptualization of racism as structural and systematic versus defining racism as individually based allows educators to reconsider, deconstruct, and form new understandings of two crucial assumptions that underpin racism as structure: colorblindness and meritocracy. These two key ideologies circulating within society afford racism its cloak of invisibility, allowing racism to avoid being overtly identified, named, and subsequently disrupted. A colorblind perspective refuses to address race, and views any "race talk" as inherently racist, thus avoiding racism and racial inequality altogether. According to Bonilla-Silva (2006), the notion of colorblind racism informs many white teachers' and administrators' attitudes and beliefs toward teaching in schools, along with an avoidance of bringing social justice into the classroom. The sharp juxtaposition between the belief many white teachers hold about racism today and the experiences of structural racism many teachers and preservice teachers of color continue to endure illustrates the dangerous power of a colorblind ideology (Modica, 2015). The notion of colorblindness, according to social justice scholars, functions as a means of upholding white supremacy within education through the denial of "color differences": differences of ethnicities, cultures, backgrounds, histories, and identities. When colorblindness is embraced by white educators and policymakers, differences in cultural capital that could enrich the learning environment and present students of color with culturally relevant and sustaining curricula instead become suppressed by whiteness rather than valued and promoted through a social justice agenda (Yosso, 2005).

Thus, colorblindness is institutionalized when issues of race and racism are removed from educational "conversations," leaving the current racialized gap in "academic achievements" unproblematized and/or understood as the result of the failure of schools and teachers. However, schools in predominantly white communities that have high scores on standardized academic tests typically are not presented with the chance to problematize the role of whiteness that might privilege those who make up the schools. Predominantly white school populations (e.g., teachers, students, and administrators) often lack the language and conceptual framework necessary to even begin to problematize whiteness. Moreover, teachers and administrators in predominantly white schools frequently avoid opportunities to understand how complicity with a lack of a social justice agenda to support diversity actually homogenizes the school curriculum in detrimental ways. This means that, for example, when white teachers lack self-awareness about racial inequality, their views, actions, and attitudes are usually coded in colorblind terms, without acknowledging and understanding how the role of whiteness informs their beliefs. The rising rates of residential segregation is another example; when choosing to live in a predominantly white neighborhood, comments such as "the schools are better," or "the neighborhood is safer" code those communities as "race free" in opposition to communities of color, often characterized as "unsafe" or "bad."

Hand-in-hand with a colorblind perspective, meritocracy promotes the idea of equal opportunity for *all* teachers to succeed pedagogically but also as "individually responsible" for their lack of student success on academic standardized tests. However, while a meritocractic approach assumes an individually based "merit" system of rewards and relies on neoliberal ideals of self-responsibility for academic achievement, teachers of color in predominantly white schools often remain disenfranchised and marginalized. Moreover, discourses of meritocracy are often taken up by white teachers and administrators who perceive social changes in established school power dynamics as unfair, discriminating against their individual "merit." The position of meritocracy thus denies the historical contingency that has informed today's status quo of whiteness. By dismissing or silencing how structural racism has played a role on teacher performance and achievement, a meritocratic approach does not encourage teachers' engagement with and/or promotion of social change.

The Universality of Whiteness

The idea of racism as structure which inherently maintains unequal positionings for whites versus Black, Indigenous, and people of color is commonly ignored in favor of the construction of a humanistic approach to race that implicitly reinforces the dominance of the universality of whiteness (Hytten & Adkins, 2001; Leonardo, 2009). The construction of whiteness as universal is problematic because if, on the one hand, whiteness is unnamed and normalized or taken for granted in today's American society, on the other hand, whiteness as universal fails to recognize how the often-invisible structure of racism preserves social hierarchies, inequality, and ultimately, white supremacy. While during the Jim Crow era, racism was overt, tangible, and explicitly upheld through legal doctrine, the current colorblind approach to race sustained by neoliberal globalization permeates the educational system in the United States. As racial equality work advanced and became prominent with the civil rights movement, the passing of the Equal Rights Amendment, and legal victories such as the *Brown vs. Board of Education* rulings, the structures of racism started to be problematized and acknowledged to further a social justice agenda. Following the civil rights movement, new racisms started to take concrete forms through the circulation of "colorblind" and meritocratic ideologies in education, working *vis-á-vis* hidden means to maintain white supremacy and white universality (Bonilla-Silva, 2006). In the past two decades, social justice scholars have advocated for research *with* and *for* historically marginalized racial and ethnic groups to reveal the "invisibility" of racism and thus, to make structures of racism visible and concrete, forwarding a social justice agenda in education and revealing how whiteness is taken for granted as the "norm."

In taking up a colorblind position, many white people might see themselves as supporters of equality (e.g., "I see everyone as equal," or "I have Black friends,") through colorblind lenses, often denying and/or feeling uncomfortable about the existence of racism as both an ideology and a structure. Even when presented with quantifiable data highlighting the inequalities between white and teachers of color in contemporary school contexts, a colorblind approach denies these inequalities as race based. This refusal to acknowledge the presence of racial inequity maintains the invisibility of racism as structure within the United States, preventing whites from engaging openly in conversations about ongoing issues of racism. In the current neoliberal era, the materiality of racism is difficult to identify, less obvious, and more challenging to critically engage with due to the acceptance of white experiences, norms, beliefs, and values as "status quo." At the same time, the materiality of racism continues to create real and wide-reaching consequences for teachers of color who work within the structures of predominantly white school contexts (Bonilla-Silva, 2015).

When history is considered, the many centuries of white supremacy in the United States as part of the foundation of the social fabric of the country have, both explicitly and implicitly, restricted access to economic and socio-educational capital for Black, Indigenous, and people of color, reducing their opportunities to pursue professional teaching careers (Milner, 2013). For instance, the link between rates of racial residential segregation and neighborhood schools is another example of the complex ways through which racism as structure works to uphold white universality. While prior to the civil rights movement, laws used to dictate where Black, Indigenous, and people of color could reside, today, these laws no longer exist. However, rates of residential segregation by race and class continue to rise, reproducing, in implicit ways, the racialization of neighborhood schools. In other words, the intersection of race and poverty as a representation of neighborhood demographics has resulted in increased school segregation, forcing teachers of color to choose between working in under-resourced schools with students of color or well-funded schools that are predominantly white. The crisscrossing of residential racial segregation, poverty, and lack of educational opportunities and access demonstrates how "racism as structure" can take place in (in)visible, complex ways through widely accepted "truths" of white universality.

In the context of schooling, when the notion of racism as structure is institutionalized in the classroom through pedagogy and curriculum, the subordinated position by teachers of color to their white teacher counterparts is produced and normalized. This racialized hierarchy is also maintained through white teachers', preservice teachers', and administrators' unwillingness or inability to name either racism, racial terminology, or white universality (Matias, 2013b). The universality of whiteness, in other words, ignores how one group (whites) can benefit from other groups' subordination or minoritization through a racialized order of teaching that places whiteness as "normal," "ideal," and at the top of the hierarchy (Gillborn, 2006; Hytten & Warren, 2003). Racialized ideologies of school curriculum are also rarely addressed by state and national curricula standards, teacher certification exams, and teachers' and teacher educators' pedagogical practices but sidestepped through coded terms such as "multiculturalism" and "diversity" (Leonardo, 2009). Educators, administrators, and policymakers' avoidance of addressing racism as structure means that they implicitly support notions of white universality as centered and invisible (Lopez, 2003).

When the notion of racism is deeply entrenched and structural in schools, it becomes difficult to conceptualize what schooling and learning might look like as a socially just institution. Similar to systems or processes such as housing, finance, the workforce, government, and the justice system, racism within education in current societal practices is not typically manifested through explicit actions (e.g., enforced school segregation or formal policies prohibiting the hiring of Black teachers). Instead, racism is implicit, thus making it challenging to articulate or address and impervious to antiracist movements and actions (Hytten & Warren, 2003). For example, taking on a colorblind perspective, many educators and administrators might view teachers and preservice teachers of color from a deficit perspective, seeing them within their communities and cultural backgrounds as disadvantaged (Matias, 2013b). In white terms, the racialized assumptions that position teachers of color as "at a disadvantage" informs the ways their identities are constructed from a "deficit" in schools—something teachers of color must "overcome" in order to achieve the "normative" position that their white counterparts perform (Kohli, 2009; Yosso, 2005). This lens of deficiency means that white teachers, administrators, and teacher educators often assume teachers and preservice teachers of color lack appropriate prior home-based knowledge and the pedagogical skills necessary for being successful in the classroom. This lens also assumes that families of color do not value or support their endeavors of teaching, and that teachers of color do not possess the socio-educational capital to advance in their teaching careers (Yosso, 2005).

Because of the widespread white Eurocentric ways of thinking about school curriculum in schools in the United States, through the lenses of a deficit model, teachers of color's cultural knowledges, experiences, and understandings of their school communities' needs are often devalued or dismissed. Many white teachers and administrators who operate from a deficit framework, for instance, might delegitimize the cultural knowledges that teachers of color poesses, lowering the standards and expectations of achievement in comparison to what is expected of their white counterparts (Gay, 2010; Ladson-Billings, 2001). Widening gaps between student and teacher racial demographics mean greater potential for cultural discordancy from white teachers, administrators, policymakers, and gate-keeping barriers (e.g., teacher certification exam, state and national professional standards for teaching, etc.). From these gaps, the institutionalization of whiteness in schools prevents white teachers from learning how to value cultures, upbringings, and histories that differ from their own, thus limiting a race-reflective approach to curriculum, pedagogies or personal beliefs. For instance, Kohli's (2008, 2009) studies showed how, through the narratives of preservice teachers of color, white teachers adopted a deficit approach to teaching students of color by constructing them in deficit terms—as "difficult" to work with, coming from "unstable" or "broken" homes, and unable to succeed academically. What white teachers ignored in their views and attitudes, according to Kohli (2008), were the structural challenges faced by students of color to be academically successful, including overcrowded classes, lack of resources and funding allocations, and pressure to perform well on standardized testing. By valuing and centering the narratives and viewpoints of teachers of color, white teachers' deficit approaches to teaching, bound up in a system of whiteness which positions students, teachers, and school communities of color as "less than" their white counterparts, are revealed, thus opening up pedagogical possibilities for social change.

WHITENESS, REVERSE RACISM, AND PEDAGOGICAL IMPLICATIONS

"Race talk" is often considered a "serious taboo" in classrooms of all educational levels, from kindergarten to higher education, leaving students, teachers, and professors without the critical tools, language, or context for thinking about, discussing, and addressing race and racial inequity (Modica, 2015). Social justice researchers have documented how, often unintentionally, white teachers, administrators, preservice teachers, and teacher educators maintain a colorblind status quo within schools and teacher preparation programs because they feel anxious about engaging in "race talk" (Levine-Rasky, 2012; McIntyre, 1997; Matias, 2013a; Sleeter, 2017). This anxiety can lead teachers to avoid talking about race in the classroom for fear of repercussions (e.g., uncomfortable or upsetting conversations with supervisors or administrators) or fear of being accused as racist. Engaging in "race talk" might also foster resentment among white teachers toward teachers of color because of the perception of being "forced" to talk about race (Matias, 2016). Yet, by avoiding any discussion or acknowledgment of race or racism, teachers are (whether consciously or not) upholding whiteness as the "normalized" academic standard. In this way, white teachers' avoidance of "race talk" reinforces a "hidden curriculum"—racialized pedagogical messages (Ladson-Billings, 2001; Leonardo, 2007; Solórzano & Bernal, 2001)—that is not explicitly identified but powerful in its underlying message of the reproduction of a racial hierarchy (Esposito, 2011).

While many white teachers might be able to recognize the potential value and importance of engaging with "race talk" in the classroom, Sleeter (2001) suggested that teachers often feel scared or unsure of how to initiate what they anticipate to be difficult or uncomfortable conversations about race with their students. For example, Modica (2015) explored a white teacher's experiences of "talking race" through a multicultural literature course, and found that the white teacher expressed significant fear and discomfort over those conversations, describing her pedagogical efforts to lead discussions of race and racism in the classroom as "risky business" (p. 401). As this example demonstrates, the negative emotions that can emerge from "race talk" might lead white teachers to avoid emotional discomfort, ultimately deciding to maintain a "race-neutral" position in the classroom (Matias, 2016).

A "race-neutral" approach is also often reproduced pedagogically by teachers' adoption of mainstream textbooks, another way of maintaining a "hidden curriculum" of whiteness. For instance, many textbooks mandated by state and district curricula fail to move beyond white-driven presentations of history, denying the account of traditionally oppressed groups' views and storytelling of their own culture, history, and struggles in the United States. Many textbooks often present a "whitewashed" version of history which maintains whiteness, racial hierarchy, and educational inequality (Perez Huber, Johnson, & Kohli, 2006). When teachers are afraid to examine whiteness and/or engage in "race talk," they then might resent having to engage in such conversations in their own classroom. In addition to their reluctance to "talk race," adopting mainstream textbooks might provide additional "whitewashed" pedagogical practices to maintain whiteness as the "norm" in schools. "Whitewashed" curricula also produce an implicit message for school community members of color that their history and lived experiences of racism are unimportant or invalid. Thus, the "hidden curriculum" can be notably detrimental for teachers of color in white schools, sending the message that the only "knowledge" worth learning in school reflects social values determined by white teachers, administrators, and policymakers (Esposito, 2011).

Problematizing and revealing a "whitewashed curriculum" in schools is crucial but social justice scholars have suggested that disrupting a meritocratic approach reassuring white teachers' white privilege is challenging (Allen & Liou, 2019; Mitchell, 2013). Holding onto the myth of meritocracy allows white teachers to continue to receive the benefits of individual "hard work," consciously or unconsciously justifying a pedagogical decision not to engage with "race talk." In doing so, notions of colorblindness and meritocracy are maintained and underpinned by the idea of "reverse racism." Reverse racism is embodied and performed when white teachers are unwilling to "talk race" because of fears of being "singled out" and judged because of their "whiteness" (McIntyre, 1997; Bonilla-Silva, 2006). White teachers, for instance, believe they experience "reverse racism" when they perceive teachers and students of color using their racial identities as a means to advance in society "unfairly," such as through affirmative action decisions (Modica, 2015).

Social justice scholars have pointed out that reverse racism is a misleading idea for several reasons (Bonilla-Silva, 2015; Cabrera, 2014; Hall, 2016; Solomona, Portelli, Daniel, & Campbell, 2005). First, the notion of reverse racism denies the implicit power dynamics upheld through the historical legacy of systematic white supremacy, and manifests as, for example, anti-affirmative action sentiments (e.g., "It is not fair that I was not accepted into this university because I am not a person of color. Why do they get all the spots?"), or as an emotional state of feeling personally attacked (e.g., "I am not a racist so it's unfair to make racist generalizations about white people."). Second, reverse racism is a false equivalency. The current imbalanced power differentials of whiteness are shaped by a history of racial inequalities that have informed current views of teaching in the United States. In turn, this power dynamic produces the cultural discrepancy between the dominant culture of whiteness permeating today's public schools and the limited access and opportunities for teachers of color to pursue a teaching profession in supportive and culturally relevant ways. Given the devastating impact of post-*Brown* desegregation efforts on teachers of color, who were demoted or fired in vast numbers, white teachers and administrators who adopt a position of "reverse racism" ignore the legal infrastructure that has historically privileged teaching as a white profession. In other words, the history of schools, teaching, and educational legislations are deeply relevant yet typically ignored when whites take up notions of reverse racism. In many schools, for instance, white teachers and administrators often espouse the concept of reverse racism by dismissing existing racial inequalities in schools and simultaneously desiring to protect white privilege. An individual's personal experiences of perceived discrimination against whiteness, or "reverse racism," fails to recognize the structural ways in which racism and prejudice toward teachers of color are still embedded at the macrolevel in today's educational system.

White teachers, administrators, and policymakers who express fears of reverse racism—whether to protect their existing power differentials or because of the perception of both threats of disenfranchisement or lack of power, thus rely on the trope of meritocracy to "address" this unfairness. Whites' endorsement of reverse racism in education highlights the dangers of a colorblind meritocracy that is based on the ontological assumption that each individual teacher should receive "merit" for their isolated actions. From a colorblind meritocratic perspective, because "equality" of access and opportunity is an integral element to the societal fabric of the United States, *all* teachers are "equal," start from an "equal" position, and thus have an "equal" chance of achieving professional success. However, the daily lived realities and struggles of teachers of color, especially when working in predominantly white schools, are not taken into account regarding notions of equality and fairness that position *all* teachers as equals in their workplace. Moreover, a meritocratic position maintains the long-lasting historical structures of legislated racism through colorblind actions, attitudes, and pedagogical practices, failing to forward a social justice agenda and challenge ongoing racialized practices in schools.

Thus, taking on the notion of "reverse racism" in schooling that positions white teachers as "oppressed" by "race" then allows white teachers to disavow or refuse to engage with "race talk" in a constructive, helpful, and positive manner. Both the centuries-old legacy of white supremacy in educational contexts and today's widespread notion of reverse racism continue to maintain teachers of color as subordinate in schools. To critically deconstruct the notion of reverse racism within education, it is important to acknowledge that, historically in the United States, Black, Indigenous, and people of color were prohibited from owning land, banned from voting, forced to attend specific, segregated, and underfunded schools, denied entry to institutions of higher education, and dictated who they could marry or were questioned as to the validity of their marriages. These examples, including legalized racist doctrine, have historically presented difficult obstacles for students of color to overcome in their desire to pursue teaching careers. Today's lack of teachers of color in schools is a consequence of how racism as structure has taken form in the United States in hidden ways, condoning the exclusion, exploitation, and marginalization of the teachers of color workforce (Leonardo, 2009). In other words, a discourse of meritocracy ignores the historical legacy of racism in education altogether and at the same time, takes individual occurrences as isolated, out of history, out of culture, or out of context. In doing so, this promotes a lens of white universality through which the idea that every teacher, no matter the color of their skin, has "equal" opportunities and access to valuable educational resources and denies the problematization of structural racism.

INTEREST CONVERGENCE THEORY TO REVEAL STRUCTURAL RACISM THROUGH POWER DYNAMICS

Along with colorblindness and meritocracy, white interest convergence is a key player in maintaining racism as structure within education, playing a powerful role in political and legal decisions on educational practices and policies. An important assumption of white interest convergence questions whether social change and racial justice are enacted when those changes benefit whites or at least do not remove or undermine white privilege. Another assumption of white interest convergence relies on the notion of a loss-gain binary approach to racial justice that aims to problematize white teachers and administrators' perceptions that advancing or progressing equity in schools can only occur at the expense, or "loss" of white privilege. While many white teachers, administrators, and policymakers can benefit from social justice work and critical pedagogies, efforts to make small-scale or localized changes in school communities are often born from a desire to protect white teachers', administrators', and policymakers' privilege and power (Gillborn, 2012; Milner, 2008).

Racial justice advances have historically been achieved through "protest and mobilization" (Gillborn, 2012, p. 6) that garner significant public and media attention, yet taking action against racism in public today might also represent a strategy to present a progressive image of "whiteness" as committed to social justice. Since the imagery of racism is tinged with a negative connotation across country and alliance lines, many of these social justice-driven actions and demonstrations are efforts to reshape a negative public image of the United States into a more socially conscious image for the global audience. In other words, white interest convergence might represent a motivation for equality and social change that does not reflect whites' altruistic commitment to racial equity or to right past wrongs but instead, a drive for staging a "democratic" image to the rest of the world. From a white interest convergence view, white teachers, administrators, and policymakers' giving lip service to promoting educational equality across racial identities is critically examined, questioning the extent to which "social progress" might occur when only viewed as beneficial for white interests and white capital (Milner, 2008).

Historically, Bell (1980) first conceptualized interest convergence theory to demonstrate how the landmark and much-heralded *Brown vs Board of Education* rulings decrying segregation as unconstitutional did not take place as a result of genuine social justice-driven intentions within education. Rather, Bell (1980) argued that whites in positions of power, including policy makers and lawmakers, saw the end of school segregation as potentially beneficial for the United States' "economic and political advances" (p. 4). Specifically, Bell (1980) theorized that to best protect white interests, assets, and power, whites' desires and opportunities for economic, political, and socio-educational capital represented the driving force in the *Brown* ruling In this vein, according to Gillborn (2012), one of the key components of white interest convergence is the notion of a loss-gain binary approach to theorize how whites' interests, assets, and power needed "protection" from an influx of people of color coming to "take" whites' economic resources. For example, using a loss-gain approach to critically examine the *Brown* ruling, social justice researchers have suggested that this ruling served as an anti-defiance mechanism to the protests, violence, and resistance to school desegregation. Additionally, Lopez, (2003) argued that the United States' global allies in the Cold War had a strong influence on the *Brown* ruling. Yet in spite of the ruling, white resistance to government-mandated desegregation in the form of implicit (vs. explicit) white-only policies implemented at the state and local level protected white teachers' access to the teaching profession, and those white-driven policies were rarely overruled by state or national courts (Bell, 1980). Bell's (1980) theorizing of interest convergence represented a useful framework to identify how a ruling which supposedly emerged from a social justice stance, in actuality, reflected the complex intersection of the "material interests of whites" with the "civil rights interests" of people of color at the time to maintain white privilege (Lopez, 2003, p. 84).

Scholars' use of a white interest convergence perspective is also beneficial when examining school desegregation efforts, where only teachers of color were brought into white schools with white students. This decision exemplifies how white policymakers and administrators begrudgingly began to desegregate schools but never at the expense of white teachers, only at the expense of teachers of color and their communities (Milner, 2008). The desegregation practice of moving teachers of color and administrators into white schools is another example of a loss-gain binary approach, in which it was assumed that the white teachers would "lose" educational capital by transitioning to work at schools serving mostly students of color. Further, a loss-gain binary is visible in district and states' ways of allocating funding for schools, often constructed as a zero-sum game, meaning that any additional funding allocation for one school corresponds to the loss of equal amount of funding for another school. Many teachers and administrators understand one poorly resourced school's funding gains in communities of color as corresponding to a well-resourced school's funding loss in a predominantly white community, and thus might be more likely to resist any conversation about racial inequalities to ensure they maintain political, economic, and social power intact (Milner, 2008).

In conclusion, the overt racism in schools and school policies that was highly visible during the Jim Crow era is absent in modern colorblind society. Yet today, race is still one of the most salient features of enduring social, economic, and political inequalities within and across educational contexts. From a white interest convergence theory, the widespread nature of the discourses of meritocracy, universality of whiteness, and loss-gain binary within schools allow social justice researchers to problematize white teachers' and administrators' lack of engagement with conversations around racial justice, especially if there is no perceived benefit for these populations from those uncomfortable conversations, and thus to continue to forward critical work for social change in education.

CRT AND INTERSECTIONALITY TO RE-CENTER TEACHERS OF COLOR

Critical legal scholarship (CLS) refers to a body of work that aims to reveal and address racialized interpretations and manifestations of legal doctrine in the United States. In particular, CLS critiques past and present doctrine as the representation or "expression of a particular vision of society" (Unger, 1983, p. 563) that has implicitly served the interests of a specific dominant group—white people. CLS was a significant forerunner in the establishment of CRT during the late 1970s and 1980s. CLS aimed to shed light on how the law is written, ratified, and interpreted as a way to uphold imbalanced power relations discriminating against traditionally oppressed groups, simultaneously de-centering and de-privileging the voices and experiences of people who hold white power. CLS as a legal movement was born out of the frustration of leftist law scholars who desired to disrupt the ideas of inherent racialized "objectivism" embedded within the standard forms of doctrine and policy in traditional legal studies (Parker, 2019). The National Association for the Advancement of Colored People (NAACP), for example, challenged the racialized interpretations of legal jurisdictions, revealing and conceptualizing the theoretical connections among racialized laws, racism, and social structures in the realms of education, government, medicine, and finance. Many CLS scholars who started their work in the law profession became the initial theorists of CRT. For instance, Derrick Bell practiced law and worked for the NAACP before he entered academia, and considered his career as a professor to be an extension of his civil rights work. In his academic position, Bell hoped to work with his students on understanding the links between social structures and racism to enhance social change and social justice in society (Tate, 1997). Bell's transition from being a lawyer to becoming a scholar aimed to shift the critical work initiated in CLS to the social sciences in academia, including educational research.

While in its historical contingency, CLS represented a form of protest against formal and legalized racism within law doctrine. The CLS movement both critiqued the conservative colorblind approach to understanding race issues and, at the same time, hoped to raise the race-conscious perspective the civil rights movement originally envisioned (Tate, 1997). As the shift from law to social sciences took hold, critical race theory (CRT) emerged as a lens and CRT scholars began to apply the underpinnings of CLS across academic disciplines—from education, to medicine, to sociology, and to finance—to theorize how race and racism play a significant role beyond the legal field and across social structures (e.g., Bell, 1979, 1984; Crenshaw, 1988). CRT scholars argued that a de-structuring of legal processes needed to take place without discounting and dismissing the negative impact of prejudice on the psychological well-being of traditionally marginalized people of color (Delgado, 1987; Tate, 1997). Because the law is a form of social control, acknowledging the intrinsic connections between CLS and CRT is important as a contextual point for understanding the origins, development, and application of CRT (Yosso, Parker, Solórzano, & Lynn, 2004). From a CRT perspective, as long as the legality of whiteness is established or legislated, implicitly or explicitly, racialized policies, racial inequality, and white supremacy will continue to be reproduced, normalized, and legalized in the institution of schooling. However, as a result of several decades of struggle, scholars' use of CRT across disciplines has established a solid research line that interrogates racism, prejudice, and whiteness from a critical theoretical lens with the intention of highlighting the racial discrepancies and systematic discourses of racism within the social structures of the United States (Bonilla-Silva, 2006; Gillborn, 2006; Ladson-Billings, 2001; Yosso, 2005).

CRT scholars have problematized dominant discourses of structural whiteness in the current public school system to critically interrogate theories of teaching and learning, and to shed light on the identities, struggles, and emotionality of teachers of color (Berry, 2005; Kohli, 2009; Ladson-Billings, 1998; Leonardo, 2009; Matias, 2016). To critically examine racial inequity and imbalanced power dynamics in education, scholars draw from five core tenets of CRT (Kohli, 2009; Solórzano & Bernal, 2001). The first tenet of CRT posits race and racism as central factors in maintaining a racialized hierarchy of whiteness within social systems such as schools (Ladson-Billings, 1998). From this position, CRT argues that it is vital to recognize the intersection of racism with other forms of prejudice and domination such as sexism, homophobia, heteronormativity, classism, ableism, and religious minoritization, along with the intersectionality of those social categories (Gillborn, 2015). The second tenet of CRT addresses the need to challenge majoritarian stories—stories of whiteness that become widely accepted narratives of experience and taken for granted as "true," even if those stories only reflect the ways of seeing life as a single dominant group. This tenet is particularly advantageous for revealing whiteness and destabilizing discourses of colorblindness and meritocracy, arguing for the need to disrupt institutionalized whiteness, to challenge majoritarian narratives, and to reveal hidden forms of structural racism embedded in many facets of the United States (Ladson-Billings, 1998). The third tenet of CRT forwards a deep and underlying commitment to social justice work to destabilize the homogenization of historically oppressed or minoritized groups. Applying this idea in educational contexts and to produce counternarratives or counterstories to whiteness toward an acceptance of heterogeneity, this tenet suggests that both schools and teacher education programs informed by whiteness should require a commitment to social justice. In particular, teachers need to incorporate antiracist approaches and pedagogies to open up possibilities for a transformational reconceptualization of school curricula (Gillborn & Ladson-Billings, 2010; Tejeda, Espinoza, & Gutierrez, 2003). To work against homogenization and essentialism, this tenet is also informed by the intersectionality of social categories to reveal how multiple local sites of oppression intersect at the macrolevel, impacting marginalized groups in negative ways (Crenshaw, 1991). Because voices and counternarratives can challenge the racialization process and sustain social justice and social change, the fourth tenet of CRT emphasizes the importance of storytelling and experiential knowledge. Storytelling uses oral history to highlight the historical connections between many racially marginalized teachers' pedagogies and curricula to their experiences, knowledge, and views, validating these stories within their own communities (Solórzano & Yosso, 2001). Counterstories allow for social justice to emerge within and between dominant narratives of whiteness, legitimating people of color's lived realities and ways of knowing and understanding the world. Finally, the fifth tenet of CRT embraces an interdisciplinary approach, challenging the construction of traditionally oppressed groups in homogeneous and categorical terms and thus highlighting the multidimensionality of the world and the vast range of experiences within marginalized groups as heterogeneous, multiple, inconsistent, and plural (Bowleg, 2012; Gillborn, 2015). This tenet provides a means of recognizing how racialized identities reflect an "intersectionality with other forms of subjugation," in which various "axes of oppression" meet at different times and places (Solórzano, Ceja, & Yosso, 2000, p. 63).

While CRT is primarily concerned with race and racial inequity as structural barriers inherent within the United States, an intersectionality framework takes into account other intersecting forms of (dis)empowerment by developing an understanding of the "complexities and multidimensional nature of oppression," from which "potential for societal change" (Cole, 2009, p. 568) can emerge. From an intersectional perspective, the notion of "difference" is reconceptualized in positive terms, while challenging the pervasive dominant discourse of "fearing difference" (hooks, 1986, p. 135). Thus, intersectionality provides a useful framework to examine how multiple social categories (e.g., ethnicity, gender, socioeconomic status, sexuality, (dis)ability, and religious affiliation, among others) intersect at the "micro level of individual experience" and at the same time, shed light on how "multiple interlocking systems of privilege and oppression at the macro, social-structural level (e.g., racism, sexism, heterosexism)" take root in society (Bowleg, 2012, p. 1267).

Through the lenses of the intersectionality, social justice researchers can highlight how overlapping social identities are constructed, reproduced, and operationalized to maintain existing power imbalances that implicitly sustain "racism as structure" (Bonilla-Silva, 2006; Bowleg, 2008; Solórzano & Bernal, 2001). By employing an intersectional perspective, scholars, researchers, and activists aim to make visible the "complex political struggles" and power relations of the "multiple positionings that constitute everyday life" for teachers of color in white schools (Phoenix & Pattynama, 2006, p. 187). Given that key elements of intersectionality aim to reveal how an individual's social identities are interdependent and multidimensional, there is an urgent need to produce counternarratives to whiteness, exploring the experiences, stories, and identities of teachers from multiple historically oppressed groups in schools (Bowleg, 2012).

Thus, to reveal how dominant discourses of colorblindness, meritocracy, and white universality impact the identities of teachers of color, an intersectionality perspective can be useful to address the racialization and minoritization of teachers of color in schools (Gillborn & Ladson-Billings, 2010). Drawing from CRT, intersectionality aims to construct race as a verb, identifying and problematizing acts of racialization and minoritization that construct teachers of color as "other" or as "outsiders" against the centered position of whiteness. Intersectionality positions whiteness and race in performative terms, recognizing how individuals can perform "race" or perform "whiteness" in multiple, fluid, and inconsistent ways. If racial identities and whiteness are performative, then the acts of racializing, homogenizing, and minoritizing "other" teachers can be disrupted, and the layered meanings of race constructed in white terms and imposed on the identities of teachers of color can be challenged. Considering schools as an institution of socialization where teachers, implicitly or explicitly, enact the "hidden curriculum," through the lens of intersectionality, teachers of color storytelling their experiences and sharing their identities provide valuable first-hand accounts of struggles for social justice and social change which disrupt whiteness in education.

CONCLUSION

While schools and teacher education programs struggle to develop race consciousness, there is a pressing need to continue to challenge whiteness as the status quo in spite of giving lip service to themes like "diversity" and "multiculturalism." In response to the current preservation of whiteness within the teaching profession, it is crucial for scholarship to examine, support, and understand the potential for the agency and empowerment of teachers of color through an intersectional CRT lens in an attempt to promote a critical consciousness within racially oppressed teaching populations (Allen, 2015). By employing an intersectionality perspective to study the experiences of teachers of color, scholars and educators may better understand how to raise critical awareness and develop critical consciousness in the classroom, assisting teachers of color in rejecting dominant discourses and creating more inclusive and culturally relevant teacher education programs and schools (Jennings & Lynn, 2005).

Understanding the struggle, agency, and empowerment of teachers of color represents an effort to move beyond simplistic conceptualizations of racialized oppression as well as a resistance to "othering" discourses (Baez, 2000). While it is not uncommon for themes of victimization and marginalization to emerge from research on racial oppression in education, using intersectionality as an analytical tool offers scholars a means of reconceptualizing these ideas of "victimization" toward agency and resistance, both of which are central themes within this theoretical perspective (Amos, 2016; Carter, 2008; Kim, 2001; Rodriguez, 2011). As such, the storytelling tenet of CRT is a crucial component of resisting discourses of colorblindness, meritocracy, and white universality in schools. By acknowledging the emotional, personal, and meaningful ways in which marginalized populations "challenge and disrupt normative narratives of the dominant group" (Rollock, 2012, p. 72), storytelling and story-sharing by teachers and preservice teachers from historically marginalized groups serve to destabilize racial inequality. From a CRT perspective, it is vital to center the counternarratives of teachers and preservice teachers of color as valid ways of understanding themselves, their experiences of racism within educational contexts framed by whiteness, and the emotionality of a racialized and minoritized identity (Matias, 2013a,b). Sharing the stories of teachers of color can make visible their identities and struggles to challenge the racialization of the "other" in school, to reveal the "hidden curriculum" of whiteness and racism as structure in educational contexts, and to lead to a better understanding of how to engage in effective social justice and antiracist work within schools.

Chapter 4

"Eye-Opening . . ."

Bearing Witness to Whiteness in School

ABSTRACT

Within the prevalent discourses of colorblindness and white universality in today's public schools, teachers of color often endure isolation, marginalization, and discrimination (Amos, 2016; Kohli & Pizarro, 2016; Simon & Azzarito, 2018, 2019). Yet, facing oppression, many teachers of color are also able to reframe their embodied identities and lived experiences from oppressed to empowered (Kim, 2001; Rodriguez, 2011; Solórzano & Bernal, 2001). This chapter presents the narratives of eight Black, Latina, and Asian female teachers located in predominantly white schools as active agents who recognized, named, and negotiated whiteness in multiple ways, as well as resisted their racialized position as the "other" in their schools. By "speaking up" about race issues and promoting "race talk" in their schools, the teachers "bore witness" to racialized oppression. The Black, Latina, and Asian female teachers thus rejected the embodiment of a "victim role" and instead engaged in varying forms of transformational resistance in response to race issues, interrupting the silence and invisibility of whiteness (Yosso, Smith, Ceja & Solórzano, 2009).

Discourses of whiteness, including colorblindness, meritocracy, white universality, and white interest convergence, all work together to maintain a silent status quo on the "othering" of teachers of color. As a result, teachers, preservice teachers, and teacher educators (e.g., academic faculty) of color may draw from their personal lived experiences and embodied identities to understand school as a place of social isolation, marginalization, and discrimination, and find themselves alone in their own teac hing settings, having only a very few fellow teachers of color working alongside them (Amos, 2016; Berry, 2005; Kohli & Pizarro, 2016; Levine-Rasky, 2000a,b;

Mogadime, 2008; Simon & Azzarito, 2018). According to several scholars (Carter, 2007; Davis, Vakalahi, & Scales, 2015; Matias, 2013a), the effects of the experiences of long-term marginalization and isolation in work settings can result in increased stress, anxiety, long-lasting emotional scars, and even physiological health problems such as hypertension, depression, and panic attacks. Across the spectrum of educational upbringing, from early experiences as elementary, middle, and secondary school students, to enrolling in teacher education programs, to then becoming in-service teachers, the lived experiences of teachers of color in school contexts frequently include many cultural barriers to overcome in order to achieve academic and professional success. In spite of those barriers, drawing from their own experiences of oppression, teachers of color often choose to pursue a teaching career with the intention of changing inequitable schooling environments and giving back to underserved communities (Hilliard, Perry, & Steele, 2003; Irizarry & Donaldson, 2012; Kohli & Pizarro, 2016).

Further, teachers of color who are located in predominantly white schools often witness white colleagues enacting "white privilege pedagogy," creating a school environment where ignorance, an unwillingness to engage with "race talk," or a lack of racial awareness, are taken for granted and normalized (Ladson-Billings & Tate, 1995; Levine-Rasky, 2000a; Sleeter, 2017). As teachers draw on notions of meritocracy and equal treatment in their pedagogies, when these pedagogical acts of whiteness are "normalized," the racialized experiences of teachers of color and work toward racial equity are dismissed. By reinforcing the notion that those who fall outside the borders of the accepted white norms of teaching and learning are "different" or "outsiders," teachers and administrators implicitly reproduce and uphold the underpinnings of white supremacy within education (Gay, 2010; Ladson-Billings, 2001; Tatum, 2017). Due to homogeneous school contexts informed by whiteness, the "othering" process might impact the identities and experiences of teachers of color in detrimental ways. It is evident that there is an urgent need for increasing the diversity of the teaching population, but also a need for the expansion of the implementation of critical pedagogies in schools in order to foster an educational environment that is intentionally antiracist and potentially transformative of educational inequity.

As a result of the "othering" process, teachers of color are marginalized within predominantly white school contexts, which can lead to struggles with identity affirmation, but also the development of racial awareness and the use of critical agency in order to challenge and negotiate whiteness in their workplaces. Creating schools that promote racial awareness might help teachers redefine classrooms as educational sites that embrace and sustain a social justice agenda (Baez, 2000). Thus, this chapter shares eight Black, Latina, and Asian female teachers' "small teaching moments" from their experiences working in predominantly white schools. The first section of the chapter offers a snapshot of the teachers' contexts and identities, and then shares how their acts of "speaking out loud" about their views, upbringings, and experiences offered an autonomous pedagogical means for the teachers to "bear witness" to racialized incidences and meaning makings. The second section discusses how the teachers, through the process of "speaking up," "opened their eyes" and named how whiteness marked their identities in school, ultimately creating a space for enacting transformational resistance.

NAMING AND BEARING WITNESS TO INVISIBLE WHITENESS

Within the teachers' varied experiences of working in predominantly white schools, there were underlying themes of racism, stereotyping, and discrimination but these forms of oppression were not foregrounded in how they understood their lives as minoritized members of their professional communities. Instead, the teachers embodied agency and autonomy within their school settings in a multitude of ways, giving voice to the call for greater understandings of the experiences of teachers of color as part of a broader social justice agenda in schools. The Black, Latina, and Asian teachers' narratives shared in this chapter demonstrate how, in spite of their marginalized positions in predominantly white schools, they were able to make sense of their embodied selves *beyond* a framework of whiteness. In general, the teachers rejected notions of victimhood and, instead, enacted a critical agency to negotiate and resist white-laden rhetoric, thus naming, or "bearing witness," by enacting critical agency in response to their experiences within their teaching contexts (Boler & Zemblyas, 2003; Bryson, 2017; Yosso, Smith, Ceja, & Solórzano, 2009). All names represented in these chapters are pseudonyms to protect the teachers' anonymity.

Participants and School Contexts

The teachers represented a wide range of backgrounds and identities (see table 4.1), although many came from working-class, immigrant families. A collective linking thread was that they all worked in elite, predominantly white, independent schools in a large urban city in the northeastern part of the United States. Criteria for inclusion as a "predominantly white school" were schools that had 80 percent or higher populations of white teachers, administrators, and students.

Kristi (figure 4.1) was first-generation Chinese American, the oldest of the participants, and had worked at her school for over forty years, serving as the

Table 4.1   Teachers' Background Information. Credit Mara Simon.

Name	Racial or Ethnic Identity	Number of Years Teaching	Roles Served during Career
Kristi	Chinese	41	Lower school program chair, teacher
Jade	Trinidadian/White	16	Athletic director, teacher
Erika	Honduran	10	Athletic director, teacher
Sasha	Black American	12	Teacher, curriculum coordinator
Celia	Black American	8	Teacher
Alicia	Filipina	8	Teacher
Natasha	Haitian	3	Teacher, athletic trainer
Serena	Black American	2	Teacher

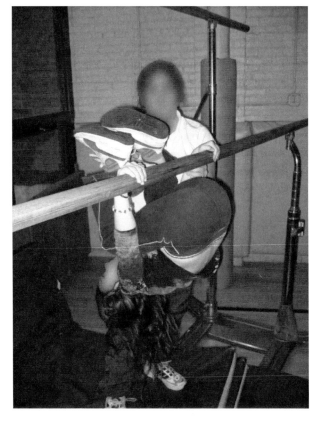

Figure 4.1   Kristi's Self-Representation, Teaching Gymnastics at Her Predominantly White School. Credit Mara Simon.

program chair for the last decade. Kristi described how her Chinese immigrant parents encouraged her to assimilate into American culture by requiring her to attend predominantly white schools as a student, which ultimately led to her working at one of the top private schools in the city since whiteness in schools had been normalized throughout her life:

> I don't know how much my parents pushed us with the fact that we were Chinese. They didn't insist that we learn Chinese. . . . They wanted us to fit in. They didn't want us to be perceived as different. . . . The schools I attended were mostly white and privileged. I felt not part of it, yeah. Not being white, I felt it, growing up. And they [white students] teased me about being Chinese . . . I think why I teach at a white school is because culturally, growing up, I was not pushed toward Chinese but toward the white culture. So I think that allowed be to look at Waltor [pseudonym] as just a school, rather than a "not Chinese" school.

Jade, who was half Trinidadian and half white Canadian, was in her second year in an administrative role at the time of the interviews at a newly constructed international school after having been a teacher for more than fifteen years prior to starting this position. Jade described how she started on her path to becoming a teacher:

> One day my mother—my mom's white, and we were watching a documentary. And in the documentary, they said that there are not many Black teachers. So we looked at each other like, "Oh my god, this is what you're going to do." So sure enough, I told some people at the university, some faculty, and they gave me a scholarship. There was actually a $1,000 scholarship for any Black student who wanted to go into education.

Erika, who was born in Honduras but moved with her mother to the United States when she was just two years old, served in a similar role as Jade as both a teacher and an administrator in her school. The school was religiously affiliated but "progressive" and "liberal," located in the downtown section of the city. Due to her increased visibility as a Latina teacher and administrator, Erika saw herself as a mentor for students and teachers of color at her school and aimed to facilitate greater diversity within her staff:

> I feel like I could be a mentor where I am, you know what I mean? I'll meet with, let's say, teachers or coaches of color or females, and they'll just gravitate toward me and just kind of accept me without even knowing me. And just because I'm of color. But I also like to focus on our kids here and making sure that our teachers or coaches are also of diverse cultural backgrounds, so they can relate to them. So that, to me, is important for everyone to get supported.

After having worked at her school for eight years, Sasha (figure 4.2), who was Black and whose family had been in the United States for multiple generations, was, during the course of the interviews, finishing her final year at her current school before moving across the country to a new city and to start working at a new school. She explained:

Figure 4.2   Sasha's Self-Representation—at the Beach, "Happy and Free." Credit Mara Simon.

I get a lot of negative feedback from administrators [here], I don't know why. I have these theories and it's not because they've [administrators] actually visited my class and seen anything, it's just based on hearsay and things that they've heard, which you know, turns out to be fabricated or exaggerated stories. So I don't feel supported in that way.

Celia, another multigenerational, United States-born Black teacher moved to her current location after being displaced from her historically Black hometown city by a major natural disaster. She described the transition from her hometown to the urban metropolis where she lived now, immediately following the natural disaster:

> That's why I moved here. I was in [name of the northeastern city] with no winter jacket whatsoever. My entire family lost everything. My grandmother was 66, and she had a stroke at the hotel we evacuated to and she passed away. That was ten years ago, so I was 26. I came to [name of city], and from there I was looking on Craigslist, and I found a part-time job here at Sampson [pseudonym]. At the time, it was just all I needed. And then from there, [an administrator] offered me a job fulltime to teach that January.

Alicia identified as Filipina American and was the second teacher of the group whose career was in transition. She was preparing to leave the school she had taught at for three years to go teach at a public school, a long-standing dream of hers after nine years of teaching at private schools. She stated:

> To be able to teach in a setting where, you know, it helped raise me, because public schools is what raised me. And I would love to just be able to be on the other end of it and teach, and in a way give back but also in a way, just learn something different. Because the private school world, it's obviously completely different from what you would experience in a public school.

Natasha was an early career teacher, in her third year of teaching, and Haitian American. She was born and raised in a highly diverse, low-socioeconomic status neighborhood at the outskirts of the city and had both attended and taught at predominantly Black and Latinx schools her entire life, all of which contrasted sharply with her current teaching job at a very prestigious, predominantly white, independent school. Natasha described this transition, saying:

> I just had to kind of learn how everyone was. I just know that I often feel a little uncomfortable [at the school].

Finally, there was Serena, who was Black and multigenerational United States-born, and just starting out in her teaching career at a predominantly white independent school. Serena (figure 4.3) viewed her job as extremely important, both to break down stereotypes of Black teachers for her white students and to serve as a role model for her students of color, so that all could witness the success story of a Black female teacher:

> I just like the kids to see someone of color that's actually positive and not what's out there in the news and in the media. Yeah, there are some people of color

Figure 4.3   Serena as an Undergraduate at an HBCU, where She Engaged in Community Service Work and Aimed to be a Role Model. Credit Mara Simon.

who are just—they're good, they have their degrees, they're doing a good job, they can actually teach. *They [students] need to see an educated Black female.*

As these initial introductions demonstrate, it was clear that within the teachers' narratives, their racial and cultural identities were a salient point of reference in how they made sense of their position as minoritized teachers within predominantly white school contexts.

Engaging with "Race Talk"

The eight Black, Latina, and Asian teachers all identified and vocalized "small teaching episodes" that illustrated how they negotiated a racialized identity against a backdrop of whiteness, thus "bearing witness" to the racialization process. Then, as the teachers shared their experiences and spoke aloud their thoughts, they started to develop racial awareness, making sense of their experiences critically and critiquing the normalization of whiteness (Bernal, Burciaga, & Carmona, 2012). "Speaking aloud," in these cases, was conceptualized as acts of "bearing witness" to the ways in which whiteness impacted their identities; the teachers often took time and reflection to be able to identity and name whiteness (Ward, 1996). For example, Jade shared how as an adult, she finally understood the many thinly veiled incidences with "race" she experienced throughout her childhood, teenage, and college years:

> I know all these little things . . . like, kids made fun of me and wrote me hate letters, or going over to friends' houses and the parents would clearly not be excited that I was there or we'd have to play outside . . . being labeled a "Rotunda Rat" in high school even though I was a straight A student, star athlete, valedictorian, my guidance counselor telling me to apply to vocational and technical school. No! I went to one of the top schools in the city! . . . Stuff like that but the fact that I remember it all . . . I mean, now in my forties, I'm like, "You know what? It was because I was Black." Like, *I figured it out*, you know?

As Jade shared this revelation aloud, she started to actively reconstruct her prior life experiences as a student in school, critically interrogating the normalized lenses of whiteness which framed these experiences. Jade's realization of "little things," such as receiving "hate mail" from a classmate, the racism of her white friends' parents, and unprompted bias and stereotyping from her guidance counselor, led her to be able to name whiteness and amplify her experiences of race-encounters. Similarly, Alicia, whose parents moved to the United States from the Philippines before she was born, described a job interview episode she understood as culturally inappropriate. Alicia reflected on the experience afterward, and explained:

> I went on this interview and the superintendent even made a comment saying something along the lines of like, "Are there teachers in your family?" And I said, "No, actually it's just my brother and my sister and me. We don't really have anyone that we looked up to that wanted to make us be teachers." And he said, "Well, is anyone else in like, the physical education realm . . . your siblings?" And I said, "No, it's just me." And he goes, "Isn't that funny? Like a female of your . . .," he said, because we were talking about the diversity of the community.

It took Alicia time to make sense of this interaction. She later explained that in her view, the white male superintendent's comment—"Isn't that funny?"

"othered" her sense of self as an Asian American female physical education teacher. According to Matthews (2002), stereotypes of Asian women construct women as subservient and passive, characteristics which contrasted with the superintendent's expectations as he relied on these stereotypes during the interview. Alicia also shared her growing awareness of an episode in her school she viewed as unfairly racialized. As she described, her school's administration singled her out, along with a few other teachers of color, by asking her to represent the school at the *People of Color Conference,* a conference specifically for teachers and students of color:

> I mean they kind of cornered me into going. I had heard about it [the conference]. Then I received an email with just three other females of our faculty who also were people of color, asking us to "consider" going to this conference. And three out of the four of us decided to go. One of them was Indian, she's a learning specialist there. Another one was Black, she taught math and physics, and then me. I had already previously considered it and I just thought, "Nah, I don't really want to go. I don't really want to like, oversee ten high schoolers." And I think it was also just a busy time. I was coaching basketball at the time, like, it would be the wrong time to go. But then I got that email. And so I showed it to my white coworker and I said, "Does this mean I have to go? Are they asking me to go?" And she was like, "Well, it's only the four of you on there, so I'm assuming they're hoping that at least one of you goes." So I reached out to those other women and I said, "Are you planning to go to this?" And they all thought it was weird too, about like why are we the only ones on the email? I felt like I was asked to go there [to the conference] based on the color of my skin.

Alicia problematized being asked to go to the conference by the administration as reflective of the school's "multicultural" approach to professional development, questioning whether she was being "singled out" because of the "color of her skin," one of a few teachers of color among a predominantly white faculty at the school. Alicia felt that only asking the small population specifically consisting of teachers of color to attend the conference was an issue because it put the onus of responsibility for social justice work and racial inequity onto her as a Filipina teacher and highlighted her as an "other," distinct and separate from her white teacher counterparts.

Serena described both the inherent "othering" she experienced as a Black teacher in a predominantly white school but also the importance and value of her presence within the school to make sure her few students of color could see positive representation of an empowered Black teacher identity (Ward, 1996). She said:

> And I always felt like there's a possibility I might be judged right at the door because I'm Black, "You probably just don't know as much," you know? In the

beginning it was real hard because I was like, "They [students, teachers, and administration] are probably not going to like me. They're probably not going to be open to anything I have to say or do here. And this going to be a struggle." And toward the end [of the year], the kids [of color] was all like, "We want you to stay. You understand us better." I think a lot of it came from the fact that I was African American. They had a few Black classroom teachers . . . and stuff like that, but *there's not a whole lot of me floating around*. I started to get it, little by little. Like, I get it, *I need to be in there*. The Black kids need to know who I am.

Serena understood that the connections between Black teachers and students in white majoritarian settings are an important source of validation and legitimation for both parties (Ladson-Billings, 2001), and decided to remain at the school in spite of consistently having to negotiate whiteness embedded within the learning environment. Serena also shared an image (figure 4.4) of a bulletin board she had created, which was important to her since it was a physical representation of her presence in the school. She said:

This is my first-of-the-year bulletin board, "Meet Miss Serena," because I'm still meeting [everyone]. So now they know exactly who I am.

Figure 4.4 Serena's Bulletin Board—an Introduction of "Who She Is" to the School Community. Credit Mara Simon.

Jade described how her identity as Black and female made her role as a leader in her former department difficult. Although this was never overtly verbalized by her staff, minor acts of resistance to her leadership by her colleagues served as an undercurrent of tension throughout her tenure at this previous school. She recalled:

> I have a feeling that some of that was met with some hostility, resistance, because they were there for twenty, thirty years and who was this young Black girl coming in and suddenly she's all of the boss, right? So it was really, really difficult to cultivate any kind of different culture than what was there.

During Jade's tenure as department chair at this school, she understood her racialized identity as a part of why the white teachers she supervised resisted her initiatives and leadership, implicating whiteness as a rationale for this resistance. Jade also recognized the impact of the dominance of whiteness on the few students of color who attended her current school, recalling the attrition of students of color. She continued:

> Unfortunately, students of color have left. And I've known they left because of the lack of diversity. They may not say that on their exit interview, but when they come into this office and we ask them, "Why are you leaving?" They say, "Why do you think?" And they tell us blatantly, "This [racism] is why we're leaving."

Just as Jade highlighted how the lack of diversity in her school informed both herself and her students of color, Celia, also noted how she was "the only African American teacher in the high school." Celia shared a photo (figure 4.5) of her softball team to capture the landscape of whiteness at her school, noting:

> I have not coached one African American kid in the past year, in softball or basketball.

Racial prejudice and a lack of diversity were woven into the fabric of all the teachers' daily lives, embodied identities, and experiences with school from a young age. Yet, by naming and bearing witness to a wide range of oppressive situations they experienced as teachers of color in predominantly white schools, however, they were also able to reject and critique various discourses upholding whiteness within their school contexts. This idea of destabilizing widely accepted truths is a key element of bearing witness, since it provides a means for reconstructing narratives of whiteness as harmful and oppressive rather than as normalized and revered (Bryson, 2017;

Figure 4.5   Celia as the Coach of the School's Softball Team. Credit Mara Simon.

Haviland, 2008; Matias & Newlove, 2017; Phoenix, 2009; Ward, 1996). For instance, Jade described how she vocally expressed her frustration over the school's lack of support for its student of color population to members of her administration:

> So I would go tell the Admissions Director, "This is another family we're los-ing." Even if we probably are [more diverse than some schools]. We probably are. *But that doesn't make it right.* It doesn't make it good. I think why it [diver-sifying] is so slow is, honestly, I think it was an afterthought, so they're playing catch-up as opposed to having it engrained from the beginning.

Jade's frustration on behalf of the sense of "otherness" students of color felt at her school and her subsequent direct actions, such as working with the Admissions Director, demonstrated a commitment to naming whiteness along with enactments of agency in working for change within her school.

Alicia was able to name and reject the ideas of nationalism and assimi-lation that her own parents had taken up as part of an immigrant legacy. Further, Alicia described how her parents fostered "assimilation practices" within her family when she was growing up, rarely speaking of their home country, but attempting to "blend in" with the white dominant culture. Alicia explained:

I think they [my parents] thought that it was important for us to not look back into this place [the Philippines] where we don't really know, like, "This [America] is your home. You're an American." They would go back and visit. But it wasn't something that they were trying to impress upon us, like, "This [the Philippines] is where you're from." It wasn't like that for us. It was kind of just like, "No, be proud to be an American. That's what you are." I do find myself, like, if I meet people, just anywhere in different walks of life, and they'll say, "Oh, you're Filipina. What part are you from?" And I'll say, "I'm not sure. I have no idea." You know, and then you get that feeling like, *why don't I know where I'm from?* Why don't I know where my mom was born?

Even now, in her early thirties, Alicia admitted she still knew very little about her parents' lives in the Philippines prior to coming to the United States. Alicia, however, critiqued the notions of assimilation and the "American Dream" her parents took up, rather than embracing their Filipina heritage. She recognized "being American" as problematic since the "American dream" demands an erasure of her ethnic heritage and a loss of understanding her family's cultural history. For Alicia, the denial of her family's history and the lack of knowledge regarding her own cultural background resulted in a loss of her sense of self.

Similar to Alicia's experience, Kristi explained how her parents, who came to the United States from China, faced significant racial prejudice and discrimination when they arrived in the early part of the twentieth century. Kristi viewed her parents' need to assimilate toward whiteness as a forever-lost opportunity to understand her family's culture and heritage. She said:

I think they really wanted us to become *Americanized*, to be American. Because back then, there was the whole stigmatism, if you're not white American, you're not good. You know, become as American as possible. But I guess that's it, the fact that China opened up and that even our students in our high school, we have lots of programs going there. And, you know, *they're learning more about my culture than me.* I wish I spoke Chinese because China is becoming a leader in the world. So a lot of things are going to start happening that involve the Chinese, and to know the language or the culture more would be helpful.

In this narrative, Kristi actively names both a wistful longing to better understand where her family came from as well as a critique through frustration over her white students having greater access to her Chinese culture than she does. According to Matias (2016), whiteness often embraces a thinly veiled "multicultural" approach which ultimately co-opts the cultures of people of color for its own benefit, such as in Kristi's example.

The teachers' storytelling all identified how stereotypes, the denial of their cultural background, misrepresentations, and oppressive racialized discourses were not trivial but central to the ways in which they understood their lives, experiences, and made meanings from their positionalities (Amos, 2016; Phoenix, 2009). However, clearly emerging from the teachers' stories was the idea that they did not see themselves as victims of racism, or engage in self-pity or self-denial; rather, the parts of themselves they constructed as oppressed instead became a pedagogical vehicle for critique, reflection, and empowerment toward social justice (Morrison, 2008; Ward, 1996). This notion of bearing witness, by both naming *and* critiquing whiteness, connects to the idea of counter-storytelling as a valid and important pedagogical means of challenging "the political nature and racial significance of knowledge that typically positions itself as neutral" (Baszile, 2008b, p. 252; Solórzano & Yosso, 2001). In essence, bearing witness to the stories and emotional costs of homogenizing racial and ethnic backgrounds, cultures, and cultural practices within predominantly white schools might potentially "open eyes," or "make visible" how whiteness operates and infiltrates the lives and experiences of teachers of color. By sharing and validating their wide range of collective experiences with whiteness, the Black, Latina, and Asian teachers' storytelling challenged majoritarian narratives of whiteness (Bernal et al., 2012).

Shedding Light on White Neutrality and Colorblindness

The idea of addressing structural inequity within schooling at the microlevel by serving as vocal advocates for marginalized populations reflected both the Black, Latina, and Asian teachers' agency in naming existing discourses of whiteness as well as their commitment to disrupting white norms and "making a difference" (Dingus, 2008; Farinde, Allen & Lewis, 2016; Irizarry & Donaldson, 2012; Kohli & Pizarro, 2016). By rejecting and critiquing whiteness as "normalized" within a multitude of school contexts throughout their lives, the teachers experienced "eye-opening" instances of a growing awareness about the pervasiveness of white privilege in education. For example, Natasha recognized how her presence at her school meant that she served as a source of support and strength for the students of color who attended. She said:

I was imagining myself being a [Black] student and the teacher saying something that would make me upset, like, "Who would I go to?" If I said something, am I just being annoying, or is this really something that I should bring attention to someone? I could imagine being a student here and then looking around and being like, "There's nobody else here to talk to that looks like me, that would probably understand how I feel right now." So, I get it. I'm like, "You guys have rarely had that before." I had it before, I know what it feels like . . . It feels nice just to see a teacher that looks like you, it's a good example. And then a lot of students [of color] come to me because they would be like "This teacher doesn't talk to me right, and she doesn't understand, can you help me with this?" I don't like that they can't find someone to talk to that they can relate to but I was happy that I can be there for them.

Natasha understood that her students of color might experience cultural discordancy, or a lack of connections to their white teachers, and that she could help students negotiate these cultural differences. She furthered this idea by identifying the meaning that she made from attending the *People of Color Conference,* an experience which contrasted sharply with her racialized position at her predominantly white school, saying:

> I went my second year, that fall, and a lot of our students, minority students, from here went. And hearing them speak about their experience and saying things like, "It's nice to see minority teachers," I didn't think that way until I went there and heard the kids talk. And then I felt like okay, *maybe I am needed here.* It just put things into a different perspective in my head. And I felt better about teaching here after going to that conference because I was really thinking about looking [for a new job].

Natasha's experiences of dominant norms of whiteness within her school were almost enough to make her want to leave the school altogether but after students expressed the importance of her role and visibility at the school, she realized that her presence was making a difference for her students of color after all.

In another example, Sasha discussed how she struggled to negotiate whiteness and white norms implicit within her school. She described this struggle as both a learning process and a chance to make a difference within her school context, saying:

> [I'm learning] how to cope, how to deal, how to be the only person in a room full of people who are not like you, how to still keep your strength, to be who you are, how to instill programs that will help the school grow [and] make people a little more open and aware about life.

Sasha recognized the harmful impacts of whiteness on her sense of self but also acknowledged the need to try to help people become "more open and aware about life," and in particular, about the norms of whiteness which were often rendered invisible in her school. Similar to Sasha's struggle to "see" herself recognized and authenticated, in another example, Kristi described how, during a professional development activity with the teachers of her school, all the faculty were asked to answer questions about their experiences related to race and then physically placed themselves in a line-up. Kristi described:

> We did one activity where we had to answer a bunch of questions, and depending upon your total number of "yes" or "no" answers, you had to stand in line.

And then we stood there and we looked at the line, there were probably 75 of us, if not 100. And you could see the whites all the way down and then it started to get different nationalities, color, races, and then toward the end of the line, it was predominately Black. And it was an eye-opener for the white faculty, like, "Wow," even at Waltor school [pseudonym], who, we're more affluent, where we provide for our staff, it was obvious. So obvious . . . that even though we have other people, we do not accept them. You know, the Black kids still sit together in the cafeteria. We don't teach much about Black, Asian, or Latino history, for example. We [people of color] still stand out. There is not that support, we do not offer support to our community that needs it. And I think that is the whole thing, that it is not socially comfortable. We still have the culture of divide.

Kristi deemed the professional development activity a hopeful wake-up call for some of her white colleagues—that the line of teachers captured the significant differing experiences of teachers of color in contrast to the white teachers at her school, and that the white teachers might then start to have some idea of what the school was like for teachers and students of color, positioned against a backdrop of whiteness.

Having to negotiate whiteness was a common experience among participants. Like Kristi, whiteness was also captured by Alicia's picture (figure 4.6) of herself with some coworkers, noting how the teaching population at her school was mostly white. She said:

People would say that all the time as a joke that our entire lower school [teacher population] was all white, at one point, even majority blonde and white.

Alicia shared this photo to exemplify the normality of whiteness firmly established within her school. For Jade, the institutionalization of whiteness as the dominant culture in her school often resulted in her fellow teachers avoiding or ignoring race altogether (Matias, 2013a; Gallagher, 2016; Sleeter, 2017):

I might be looking around and seeing, "Okay, there's six of us. I can count how many women of color there are here," which can be kind of disheartening, right? Now I'm trying to think how many of us are there. But I mean, it's the opposite [for them]. Like say you're a white male or a white female, you don't even have to have that conversation. You're not going to say, "How many of us are there?" You lose count. I mean, *I* know there's 200 of you.

While whiteness dominated the teaching landscape at Jade's school, however, in this discussion, through the naming and critiquing of whiteness, Jade actively "opens her eyes" to positions of marginality in her predominantly

Figure 4.6   Alicia with Her Coworkers. Credit Mara Simon.

white school. She also shared an image of a very large painting (figure 4.7) she had hanging up in her office, which she viewed as another form of rejecting her marginality, saying:

> The *negra morenas* [Black women], my *tres chicas* [three women] painting is just so special to me. So I made sure I brought it here.

The visual representation of Black women in the painting upends images of whiteness carefully coded throughout the school, demonstrating Jade's commitment to highlighting and making visible the experiences of students, teachers, and administrators of color.

One key means in which whiteness is normalized and racism is invisibilized (and thus subtly condoned) within schools in the United States is through discourses of racial neutrality or colorblindness (i.e., an inability or unwillingness to "see" race or racial inequity). CRT scholars and antiracist educators have problematized forms of "racial neutrality" in favor of "speaking up" about racial experiences and inequality openly and directly (Bonilla-Silva, 2006; Ladson-Billings & Tate, 1995; Leonardo, 2009). In this chapter, teachers' talking about race created a space for them to reflect upon the many forms of colorblind interactions they had encountered in their upbringing and professional careers. This safe, intimate, and supportive space also created means of personal growth as well as development of critical awareness and

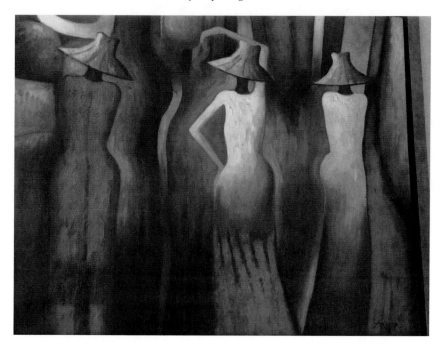

Figure 4.7   The Painting in Jade's Office. Credit Mara Simon.

critical consciousness, as many began to recognize how discourses of color-blindness or white neutrality had permeated their experiences. For example, Alicia described how, when growing up, her family simply ignored race, despite standing out as a Filipina family residing in a predominantly white suburb of a major metropolis. While socioeconomic status was not a notice-able "difference" since her parents were college educated and working pro-fessionals, being Filipina meant she stood out among her white community and she started to recognize how "race talk" was a taboo topic for her family and community. Alicia explained:

> So I mean it was never really a big deal to me, like race/nationality/color. It was just never huge and never something we really even spoke about at home. And maybe that—*maybe that's a fault*, you know? Like, *maybe we should have been a little bit more aware growing up* . . . I think this whole experience has helped me to reflect on all my years of growth and learning more about myself. I feel like our interviews, the questions, really brought me back to places where I'm like, "Wow, is this really how it started?" And even after I leave here, I start thinking about the things that I just talked about, how meaningful, these ques-tions have forced me to like dig down deep so that everything that comes out is valid. And it's valid and it's so real and it's so raw. I feel like it's really helped

me grow as a professional. This has helped me a lot to know what I want in life
and where I want to go in the future.

Alicia's reflective words suggest the possibility for future engagement with a
critical awareness and consciousness around the role race played during her
youth, growing up in a predominantly white community, as well as her for
her future career as a teacher.

Similar to Alicia's experience of whiteness but identifying from an ethnically different cultural background, Kristi's family of Chinese immigrants
silenced race when she was growing up in the 1950s and 1960s. For the
United States, this period was historically a time characterized by heightened suspicion towards China due to fears of communism and the Cold War
(Brickner & Hanson, 2003). Kristi said:

> I mean, when I was growing up, it [racism] really wasn't an issue you pointed
> out or talked about.

However, later during her teaching career, she slowly started to become
aware how issues of race and diversity came into play in her school and
appreciated the school administration's efforts to begin to address issues of
colorblindness. Kristi described her experience in her own words, saying:

> Even though we *had* "other" people, we did not accept them. Which is why
> we've gotten on to this whole diversity thing. We have, you know, workshops.
> *We meet and we talk.* I mean it's incredible what we're doing right now—
> *opening eyes.*

Kristi's words reflect a desire to be an agent of transformation for "other" students and faculty by increasing the school's commitment to racial awareness
and equity. Kristi's positionality echoes research findings that demonstrate
how enacting social change within schools is often one of the primary reasons
teachers of color decide to pursue a teaching career (Bryson, 2017; Dingus,
2008; Farinde et al., 2016; Solem, Lee, & Schempler, 2009; Williams,
Graham, McCary-Henderson, & Floyd, 2009). Kristi continued, constructing
herself as actively involved in raising awareness within her school community, challenging colorblindness or racial neutrality. She pointed out:

> It is *eye-opening.* I would think that there are some people here who go home
> and—you know, they may not admit it to the group but they might admit it to
> themselves, "*I didn't realize that the way I communicated implied such-and-
> such.*" I mean, because, you know, you look at our population of faculty. So
> white and upper class.

Rather than simply ignore the colorblind attitude of her white counterparts or perceive herself as hopelessly subjected to racist discourse (which implies an internal passivity), Kristi instead recognized and named colorblindness as problematic.

While isolation, disconnection from peers, the racialization of relationships with colleagues, and the promotion of white rationalization and objectivity often characterize the experiences of teachers of color (Baszile, 2008b; Brunsma, Embrick, & Shin, 2017; Cheruvu, Souto-Manning, Lencl, & Chin-Calubaquib, 2015; Gay, 2004), negotiating colorblindness might also become a significant source of emotional struggle for teachers of color. For instance, Celia had to actively "fight" to serve as an advisor for her students of color since she felt she could develop stronger cultural connections with them, yet experienced derision from the white teachers in her school whose colorblindness meant they could not understand or even see the meaning within these connections:

> We lack in the department of diversity. And we, as teachers, we play an advisor role and *I always try to fight for minority children*, but the other teachers kind of laugh, and it was like, "Oh, you just want her because she's Black." And in my head, I want to tell them, "Yes, I do want her because she's Black." Yes, you know, *yes*! When you guys are talking about grades and class participation in family conference, I spend an hour in a family conference, 30 minutes longer, just speaking about how it's okay to wear your hair in braids, it's okay to be from [a historically Black neighborhood], it's okay to invite some of your [school] friends to a birthday party that you're having at your apartment. So they [the students] can have someone to relate to. And just jokes, you know, around Thanksgiving time, the kids was, "Oh, I cannot wait to eat pumpkin pie with whipped cream." And one of the Black kids and I looked at each other and was like, "No, sweet potato pie . . ." Yeah, *I got you.*

Celia's desire to play a reassuring role in understanding and "seeing" or "getting" (i.e., really understanding) the lived experiences and community cultures of her students of color stemmed from the colorblind assumptions within her predominantly white school which positioned white norms and experiences as standard and anyone falling outside of these standards as an "other."

In an effort to destabilize colorblindness, Serena recognized how whiteness might work to silence "race talk," delegitimating a Black student "speaking up" about her views and experiences. Serena described an incident during a job interview at a predominantly white school (at which she ultimately was not hired), saying:

> Maya [Black student] was her name, and what she said that day in the locker room when I was in there, she came in and she said, "Are you going to be

working here?" And I said, "No, I'm just here for the day." And she was just like, "Oh, well, it's good that you're here. *It's about time that I see somebody who looks like me here.*" So one of her classmates was like, "You know, that's being racist." And she said, "That's not being racist." She was like, "Being racist is when you say something negative about someone's skin color," or something along those lines. And she was just like, "I'm just simply complimenting the fact that there is somebody here who looks like me, that I can identify with." And I was just like, "I'm proud of you for speaking up for yourself like that and good job." And you know, even with that, it just kind of confirmed things. And I'm just like, "Okay, well maybe I do need to be in this atmosphere." Because for a long time I was like, "No, I don't need to be in this [white environment]."

Serena positioned herself as an educator and ally who was willing to legitimate and support her Black student in naming and speaking out against colorblindness, thus engaging in a strengths-based approach to teaching (Ladson-Billings, 2001) that upholds and validates Black students' experiences instead of centering whiteness.

In the same manner, Jade detailed an example of how she vocalized her rejection of a racially neutral and privileged position held by several white teachers at her school. During a school meeting that aimed to address issues of diversity, Jade's colleagues consistently dismissed engaging with "race talk" and the need to include more diversity. In response, Jade confronted these white teachers' colorblind perspectives, recalling:

Because when we had a diversity awareness day here with the faculty, some of the things I was saying out loud, a lot of the lower division teachers were like, "Really?" *Like, they never believed that that could happen.* Or they were kind of *blinded*—"We need diversity here?" "I thought we were diverse enough." And I'm like, "*No!*" . . . That's my biggest challenge here, is the lack of diversity . . . They're working on it, but you know, my daughter [who attends the school], she's five and she came home the other day and she said, "Why am I the only Brown girl in my class?"

In this example, Jade challenged other teachers' views informed by whiteness, advocating for more diversity to disrupt homogeneity and whiteness in the school. According to Leonardo (2009), teachers who reject the dominant yet invisible hegemony of whiteness that maintains the experiences of white teachers as "normal" might create a space for enacting transformational resistance. The notion of transformational resistance draws from Giroux's (1983) argument that resistance which represents the intersection of an individual's critique of oppression and desire for social justice offers the greatest possibilities for empowerment.

Matias (2013a) pointed out that it is not easy to challenge status quo, particularly in professional settings or in front of colleagues, and is made even more difficult when the forms of white sensitivity and white emotionality are underpinned by a colorblind rhetoric. Thus, racially minoritized teachers' dedication to disrupting colorblind discourse demands exhausting mental and emotional work (Matias & Liou, 2015). From her critique of whiteness, Jade then connected her own personal teaching experiences to a commitment to enhancing social justice in her own community. She observed:

> I think that's probably part of the reason why I am so passionate [about] ensuring this community is a little bit more diverse, because *I know what I went through.* Just for the simple thing of like, tolerance and understanding others and *not being in your little bubble of everyone [who] looks and sounds like you* . . . You have to do an intentional outreach then. If you're seeing that they're [people of color] not applying because they say, "Hey, I'm not going to come here because there's no one there that looks like me," and we have heard that before. Or you have to go to the conferences, you have to go to the job fairs and make yourself visible and say, "Look, this is what we're about. Please come apply." If you want to be an all-white school or an all-European school, don't say you're really diverse. Don't give lip service to it. Just do it or don't market it. Don't put it in your brochures. Because if you look at the brochures, you would think, "Oh my gosh, very diverse."

Jade's commitment to the recruitment of teachers and students of color exemplifies an effort to work toward social justice, her own "conscious sense that individual and social change was possible" (Solórzano & Bernal, 2001, p. 320), and a form of transformational resistance.

The narratives shared in this chapter illustrate how the eight Black, Latina, and Asian teachers engaged with "race talk" and "opened their eyes" to homogeneity, racialized ideologies, and the normalization of "sameness" in attempts to disrupt whiteness and colorblindness (Boler & Zemblyas, 2003). In their narratives, the teachers did not position themselves as "oppressed," but forwarded a sense of "empowerment, not victimization" in their own "fight against racism [and] quests for effective social change" (Kim, 2001, p. 101). The Black, Latina, and Asian teachers in this chapter refused to passively accept the "status quo" in their schools and instead expressed vocal and active critiques of discourses of colorblindness and white neutrality, challenging school norms informed by whiteness. From their narratives, it is clear that the legitimation of a wide range of teachers' positionalities and "race talk" in schools might promote transformational resistance by teachers of color to create more inclusive and equitable school experiences.

CONCLUSION

In spite of their consistent struggles to negotiate whiteness, in this chapter, the Black, Latina, and Asian teachers spoke up to disrupt stereotypes and employed tactics of transformational resistance to maintain "strong racial/ ethnic self-definitions" (Carter, 2008, p. 489). By giving voice to their oppression, the teachers created counterstories to "formal" (e.g., white) truths and knowledges, legitimating different ways of being in school (Berry, 2005). Centering and validating the narratives of teachers of color in predominantly white school contexts challenges the notion of people of color as passive subjects who are acted upon by oppression, instead enabling the teachers to reposition themselves as active agents who engaged in "race work." As active agents, the eight Black, Latina, and Asian teachers in this study autonomously and intentionally "negotiated and struggled with structures and created meanings of their own from these interactions" (Solórzano & Bernal, 2001, p. 315; Solórzano & Solórzano, 1995). Solórzano and Bernal (2001) argue that transformational resistance within school contexts may ultimately result in social transformation, as opposed to social reproduction. The idea that resistance can be transformational challenges the common notion of self-defeating resistance by oppressed groups of people. Solórzano and Bernal (2001) explained that self-defeating resistance implicates a resistance enacted through behaviors that further isolate traditionally marginalized people of color, or "re-create the very oppressive structures they are attempting to critique" (p. 322).

According to Puigvert (2003), it is not uncommon for scholarship to represent oppressed people as "subjected to" acts of oppression or as unable to actively locate their identities within oppressive locations. However, oppressed populations often do not see themselves as oppressed but rather as able to derive meaning and purpose from an agentic position within a framework of oppression. Critical agency presents actions not as solely "free will but as actions that are possible within the context of disciplinary power" (Baez, 2000, p. 385). Thus, bearing witness and enacting critical agency might be done in the face of those who would deny or reject the empowerment of marginalized groups of people. The teachers' narratives did not present their marginalized positions as "subjected to" oppression but instead acknowledged and validated their agency, strength, and resistance for social change in schools.

Chapter 5

"Feeling Race"

Embracing Culturally Relevant, Sustaining, and Disrupting Pedagogies

ABSTRACT

The teachers' narratives in this book support the widespread call for the development and implementation of pedagogies that facilitate the integration of cultural relevance or proficiency within both schools and teacher education programs. This last chapter offers an additional narrative that intertwines, adds, and contributes to the previous eight teachers' stories. Included in this chapter is a final story told by Mara Simon, the primary researcher who conducted multiple interviews with each female teacher of color. Mara's own story as a teacher, teacher educator, and scholar offers an additional "small teaching episode"—the narrative of a white female teacher's lived experience of "feeling race" in a predominantly white school setting. Drawing from her own experience of race, Mara's narrative aims to acknowledge how difficult whiteness is to disrupt, even with an overt, long-term, and serious commitment to social justice. Critically reflecting upon the nine "small teaching episodes," including Mara's narratives, the chapter concludes by suggesting that embracing and enacting culturally relevant, sustaining, and disrupting pedagogies represent one way for *all* teachers—teachers of color and white teachers—to integrate a social justice agenda in school; for teachers of color and white teachers to deal with whiteness critically; and for teachers of color to reinsert themselves and affirm their cultural knowledge into the field of education.

The Black, Latina, and Asian female teachers' narratives included in chapter 4 provide valuable counternarratives to dominant racialized forms of schooling, calling for a social justice and equity agenda that explicitly challenges and reveals whiteness as the prevailing ideology institutionalized in many

97

schools. Reflecting upon the eight Black, Latina, and Asian female teachers' "small teaching episodes," it is clear that whiteness played a crucial role
in their daily lives and teaching experiences. Thus, against the "othering"
processes institutionalized in schools, critically reconsidering standardized
"white" normative approaches to curricula, pedagogy, and educational policy
that position teachers of color as "different" is an urgent enterprise. In spite
of their struggles in schools, the eight Black, Latina, and Asian teachers felt
a sense of empowerment, validation, and legitimation in telling their *own*
stories; and felt a commitment to negotiating power relations established by
whiteness, sustaining a social justice agenda in their own cultural terms. The
teachers' narratives call for the integration of culturally relevant pedagogies
(CRP) to reconstruct schools as crucial spaces to enact social justice teaching,
thereby cultivating agency among teachers of color and providing measures
of "success" beyond traditional, Eurocentric white educational standards.

Moreover, the experiences of the teachers included in chapter 4 support
the widespread call for the advancement and implementation of curricula that
focus on critical emotional literacies of both racialized identities and racism
as structure, facilitating cultural relevance or proficiency within both schools
and teacher education programs for *all* teachers. Specifically, critical emotional literacy on how to "feel race," (Matias & Liou, 2015, p. 619), or how to
understand the emotional impact and legacy of racism and whiteness within
schools, is a crucial tool for all teachers toward deconstructing and destabilizing whiteness within education. But discourses of colorblindness, meritocracy, and white interest convergence typically prevent pedagogical and
curricular development on the subjects of race, racism, and racial identities,
assuming that "feeling race" is not something that can be learned or taught,
especially for white teachers and teacher educators. Rather, "feeling race" is
something that should be inherently "known" since race (or lack thereof, in
the case of whiteness) is a core part of identity. However, when white teachers lack critical awareness or the appropriate cultural training to embrace
and address race, racism, and racial inequality within school settings, it is
clear that new pedagogical approaches to develop critical racial emotional
literacies would be beneficial for both teachers of color and white teachers
in schools, given the United States' rapidly diversifying student population.

To embrace the integration of a social justice agenda in education, this
last chapter suggests that the paradigm of culturally relevant teaching needs
to be seriously considered as the next steps to help white teachers deal with
whiteness critically as well as support the experiences of teachers of color
in negotiating whiteness in education. Recently, social justice scholars have
advocated for increasing diversity in the teaching population as an effort
towards enacting social change within education and facilitating equitable means of knowledge production and resource distribution for racially

marginalized populations (Gay, 2010; Ladson-Billings, 2014; Paris, 2012). In addition, using CRP as an epistemological approach to teaching facilitates teacher and student reflective practice on the emotional responses to racism and whiteness as pedagogy. This is crucial in order to provide teachers of color *and* white teachers with meaningful and critical engagement in working for social change, thus developing a critical consciousness and a means of disrupting whiteness and racism in schools.

Specifically, this chapter highlights how CRP can be used to problematize teachers' positionality, paradigms, and embodied dispositions in their specific school contexts, using critical epistemologies of race and whiteness to better support teachers of color as well as to engage white teachers with "race talk" (Aronson & Laughter, 2016; Ladson-Billings, 1995). Thus, expanding on the Black, Latina, and Asian female teachers' stories from chapter 4, the first section provides an additional story told by Mara Simon, the primary researcher and interviewer of the visual narrative inquiry. Mara's story is a reflection on how her own positionality as a white teacher, teacher educator, and scholar connects and entangles with the experiences and views of whiteness of the eight Black, Latina, and Asian teachers. In an effort to disrupt whiteness, the second section presents the key tenets of CRP, highlighting the problems with the generic forms of "multicultural education" still prevalent within education, and thus establishing CRP as a viable and research-backed approach to teaching with long-term positive effects for *all* teachers. The third section then advocates for the implementation of culturally relevant, culturally sustaining, and culturally disrupting pedagogies to integrate a social justice agenda in schools, thus empowering teachers to continue to engage in "race talk." Finally, the last section recognizes the importance of "emotionality" in the struggle against oppressive racialized school contexts and its valuable effects when implementing culturally relevant, culturally sustaining, and culturally disrupting pedagogies, thus sustaining "race work" in schools and teacher education programs.

EMBRACING SOCIAL JUSTICE FROM A WHITE TEACHER'S VIEW: THE "OTHER" SIDE

The Black, Latina, and Asian teachers' small teaching episodes are deeply important in critically embracing and understanding teachers' processes of negotiating whiteness, particularly in predominantly white schools. These negotiations are not only difficult for teachers of color but also for white teachers who are committed to social justice. Struggles against racial discrimination were witnessed first-hand by Mara Simon—the primary researcher and interviewer who conducted all the interviews with each of the eight female teachers of color. Mara identifies as a white female, and worked as a teacher in predominantly white schools for almost a decade before transitioning to teacher education at a predominantly white institution. As a white researcher, teacher educator, and former teacher, Mara's voice intertwines with the counternarratives from the Black, Latina, and Asian teachers in this book. Her story aims to amplify and contribute to the complex ways the teachers created a space for raising critical consciousness and for understanding and shedding light on whiteness within their teaching contexts from their own positionalities and teaching experiences. In the following account, Mara shares her own narrative of a "small learning episode"—a time when she first became aware of how whiteness implicitly functioned to "other" her colleague's racialized teaching positionality and experiences in a predominantly white school. Mara's narrative also aims to reveal her own colorblindness, and to offer a personal account of how whiteness and a social justice framework can collide, intersect, and/or coexist in complex ways. When Mara taught in predominantly white schools, she recalled initially being mostly oblivious and colorblind to the idea that the experiences of her colleagues who identified as teachers of color could be quite "different" from her own white privilege. However, when Mara was directly confronted with how the "othering" process was impacting her Black female colleague at her school, she started to become aware of her "raceless" understandings of white privilege and racial issues as problematic. Mara recalls:

I was new to the school, only having worked there for about two months at the time, although I was beginning my fourth year of teaching and finally starting move away from "novice teacher" status. While starting at a new work environment is always an imposing task, I quickly integrated into the school community, feeling comfortable with my role and enjoying supportive and collaborative relationships with fellow teachers. One day, as I was waiting for a class to arrive, my colleague, Sharay, who was Black, approached me in tears. What she told me next was a shock; Sharay described how she had been called into the principal's office for a meeting with several administrators, where she was scolded for her means of communication with students and told that she was being put on probation. The specifics of the behaviors that sparked this response from the administration were vague and never fully articulated to Sharay; there was no "major" transgression pinpointed during the meeting, only references to "innappropriate" tone and means of communicating. Sharay was heartbroken and spent the class crying, while I tried to recover from my surprise and still teach, inwardly reflecting on the reasons for my shock to this incident. First, since we were specialist co-teachers together, I had watched Sharay teach for almost two months and had a deep respect for her as an educator. She cared for her students, was devoted to the profession, and I had learned a lot from observing her in terms of pedagogy, class management, and lesson design and implementation. Second, in my eyes, the school's environment and administrative team had been so inviting and open that it felt hard to comprehend the idea of a formal meeting with punitive outcomes toward another teacher.

Probation is a very serious charge in independent schools, where teachers usually do not have union protection; it is one step away from being fired. I swallowed my feelings of anxiety and astonishment, and consoled Sharay in the moment as best I could, telling her that I thought she was an excellent teacher. She could only communicate her despair, surprise, and confusion, as she wondered what exactly it was that she had said to her students that was problematic enough to get her put on probation. We managed to somehow carry on with our classes and our routines of the day so it was not until later in the evening, as I reflected on the experience, that it dawned on me—this was a "real-life" example of cultural incongruence between a Black teacher and her predominantly white school as well as a real-life example of the sanctions often imposed upon teachers of color if they do not meet the "white" norms and standards of their schools. The damage of this experience on Sharay's teacher identity was immediate and long lasting; for the rest of the year, she was wary, less engaged, and slowly withdrew from her formerly vocal and highly visible position within the school. Sharay ended up leaving the school the following year as she moved across the country with the hope of "a fresh start."

In Mara's eyes, Sharay's direct communication style, often typical of Black teachers (Howard, 2001; Ladson-Billings, 1996), did not "fit" within the white school's expected modes of communication delivery. Even though Sharay paid particular attention to cultivating meaningful and supportive mentoring relationships with *all* her students—the few students of color at the school as well as caring and positive relationships with her white students—such effort did not seem to matter to the school's administration. Mara continued:

While I was only a beginner-scholar at the time, just starting my doctoral work exploring issues of structural racism in education and the need for CRP, I recognized Sharay's experience as vividly highlighting one of the reasons why there are so few teachers of color in the field, particularly in predominantly white schools—the cultural incongruence between teachers of color and their white school contexts often leads to both professional and personal sanctions and a process of "othering." What I hope to illuminate in sharing this story is the stark contrast between my own experience working at predominantly white schools, in which I felt welcomed and was easily drawn into being a part of the community, with Sharay's experience, where she consistently needed to engage in a process of negotiating whiteness, resulting in her disappearance from the community altogether.

This was not the only time Mara identified tension in the coexistence of her two identities as both a social justice scholar and white person (with the typically accompanying white privilege), as she shares:

> There are more layers to my personal narratives than Sharay's disavowal by her white school administration, although that one is quite central to my professional work as a teacher educator. However, that story is one that happened to another and I was mainly a bystander. What I will share now is an incident that demonstrates, at the intersection of my scholarly identity actively engaged in furthering a social justice agenda with my personal yet inseparable identity as a motherscholar (Matias & Nishi, 2018) trying to develop a critical conscious in two tiny humans from a very young age, how I negotiated the process of being directly confronted with whiteness and white privilege. Sharing this story represents a vulnerability for me, as it is highly emotional, but I am presenting it here in order to demonstrate the pervasiveness of whiteness in its' sheer scope, depth, and breadth and, despite my best intentions, how difficult it is to disrupt.

The following episode aims to highlight how Mara's own investment in social justice and antiracist work as a white teacher and scholar collided with her daughter's unstated yet implicitly understood alignment with whiteness. She explains:

> It's 6:45 p.m., just after we have finished up a family dinner, and my kindergarten-age daughter is inconsolable. Between sobs, she manages to squeak out that I am going to get a note from her teacher. After much prodding and several false starts, she finally tells me the reason why—she was part of a group of kindergartners who were teasing another student in her class. Instinctively and somehow, I know in my heart that there is more to this story than just school children taunting and my heart sinks as I connect her sobs to the severity of the incident. I instantly think to myself "Don't let it be Lela. Don't let it be Lela." Lela is the only Black student in her class so the odds are in my favor but deep down, internal alarm bells start ringing. At first, she refuses to tell me the name of the child of whom they were making fun. My internal monologue plays out— "Don't let it be Lela. Let this be only about bullying. Bullying, I can handle. Racist bullying? I'm not so sure." Again, after much prodding, she finally says the name: Lela. She and her three friends (all white) were taunting this student directly about her racial identity. The bile in my stomach churns as I realize my five-year-old has been the perpetrator in a racist incident at school. She, a white

child, has made fun of another child because of the color of the child's skin. I can hardly breathe.

With my daughter and with my family, we talk in further detail about the incident, and about racism and power in the United States. I explain, as I have many times beforehand and in language that is age-appropriate, how there is a long history in the United States of white people hurting people of color. My daughter knows this, themes of identifying and illustrating historical racism have always been present in my parenting. Perhaps, in some way, this conversation sinks in a little bit deeper. I explain how what she did was racist—it was an act rooted in the pain of a person of color inflicted upon by someone who is white. I connect this idea with anti-Semitism, telling her that there are also many people who want to hurt Jewish people. Therefore, as Jews, we have an especially meaningful responsibility to stand up for other people who are experiencing prejudice or racism. She sobs some more, starting to realize the violence she has inflicted on her classmate. She decides, after I ask her, that one thing she can do to make amends is to write Lela a note. I write the words for her as she dictates—"Dear Lela, I'm very sorry. I did not know this made you feel bad. Will you still please be my friend? I'm very sorry."

After my daughter is asleep, I send the teacher an impassioned email, looking for some way to be absolved for my daughter's sins, for her to tell me the incident was not as bad as I'm fearing (she responds in the morning; it was indeed as bad as it sounds). I go to bed, rife with horror and imagine what Lela's mother and father must be feeling. I also know that this is a spiral of guilt and shame that often prevents white people from moving forward in antiracist or social justice work. I try not to let my own feelings of absolute shame and terror take focus and instead, picture over and over again the pain of Lela's parents, who most likely knew, unfortunately, that this day would come and now have to face the reality of their daughter's racialized identity as a potential source of pain from enduring racism at the hands of fellow students. I feel sick over the idea that my daughter has contributed to this. I stay awake far too late into the night, wrestling with my own emotions, wondering if I have, in spite of aiming to make race "visible" through our collection of books, games, dolls, and toys as well as explicit and direct conversations about racism, somehow created a mini White Supremacist, ready to uphold the racist underpinnings of American society, to march with the KKK, and to hurt anyone who does not look like her. In spite of all my efforts toward raising "woke" children who can recognize and name systematic white privilege, here was my daughter enacting the very worst, the very explicit, the very characterized example of racism that could possibly happen.

I cycle through a multitude of strong emotions: Mortification, sorrow, desperation. I want to call Lela's parents and apologize, tell them "No, we are *not* racist in this house! This should not have happened! I work on antiracist scholarship! We read books featuring children of color! I actively talk about racism with my white children! I never took a colorblind approach!" But I force myself not to, as I know this is again, my own white guilt and privilege coming out. Why should Lela's parents have to make me feel better? They are the ones who have been hurt and my attempt to apologize or offer an explanation would only serve to center my own white feelings and white shame. But I still want to do it, even though I do not. And so, I arrive at the inevitable, exorbitantly painful conclusion—my own beloved children and my own white motherscholar self still participate in a system of whiteness from which all other identities are positioned. Thus, even as I aim with my pedagogies as a teacher educator, my child-rearing and parenting approach, my very intentions within the world, to dismantle white supremacy and to work toward equity within education and the world, I simultaneously am situated in a centered position in a world of white dominance and privilege. How do I reconcile these notions? How do I move past these intense feelings of guilt, shame, and terror? How do I make this all right?

I realize there are not answers to my questions and I am still wrestling with them, but I believe my own experience and narrative demonstrate the importance of enacting CRP for *all* students, even very young children, starting with early childhood education. Culturally relevant pedagogy in the classroom could have helped my daughter understand the implications of her words as well as re-framed her white teachers' response to the incident, which was appropriate but not as strong as I hoped. The intense difficult emotions of that night still make me catch my breath, remaining strong within me even as I write this over two years later. Matias (2016) argues that the pain of racism for white people is an emotion we avoid at all costs; it is a label that carries a strong stigma and therefore, a strong desire to detach from the idea altogether. But race, racism, and whiteness are inevitable occurrences in the lives of white people, if they choose to acknowledge their existence, even as the privilege of being white affords the choice to ignore these issues altogether. In my own experience of whiteness with my daughter, my narrative represents an example of "feeling race"; an example of how, even with my explicit commitment to social justice, negotiating whiteness from a white perspective was an emotional struggle and difficult task for me. The strong negative emotions stemming from the incident have been difficult to reconcile even as I continue to reflect on the experience of coming face-to-face with my own white privilege.

Mara's story of being directly confronted with whiteness through her daughter's participation in an overtly racist act is an example of the emotionality that very often accompanies "race talk" for white people, particularly when navigating the process of coming to terms with whiteness as a system and as a privilege. She experienced deep shame over this incident, shame which she notes has stayed with her long term, to the point where she struggled deeply with sharing the story at all. What is clear from her narrative is that there needs to be more structural means for negotiating whiteness in which the emotions of "race talk" can be processed, revealed, and ultimately disrupted. Thus, this narrative highlights a significant need for culturally relevant, sustaining, and disrupting pedagogies within institutional systems in society such as schools to present both teachers and students with opportunities to make sense of their white or racialized identities through a critical lens. The intertwining of Mara's narratives with the Black, Latina, and Asian teachers' narratives in chapter 4 represents multiple stories and positionalities within schools on how "race talk" can be impactful on teachers' understandings of themselves within an educational landscape informed by whiteness.

FROM CULTURALLY RELEVANT AND RESPONSIVE PEDAGOGIES TO CULTURALLY SUSTAINING AND DISRUPTING PEDAGOGIES

CRP means teaching in a way that honors and legitimizes the cultural capital of *all* involved in the teaching and learning process, beyond white Eurocentric school curricula, including *all* teachers. The development of a formal framework for CRP stemmed from a reaction to long-standing and pervasive deficit pedagogies toward students and teachers of color enacted, often unintentionally, by white teachers and administrators. This fundamental shift on how to conceptualize successful teaching rejected traditional Eurocentric models of teaching and white standards for student achievement, tied to beliefs on academic success, that circumvented teachers of color's sense of self and instead positioned them as "less than" their white counterparts. Ladson-Billings' (1995) critical examination of the racist underpinnings of public school education reframed teaching toward an assets-based approach, directly emphasizing cultural content as exemplars of desirable knowledge (Milner, 2017). Similarly, Gay (2010) argued for the use of teacher practices which tap into a vast "range of cultural beliefs, experiences, contributions, and perspectives . . . [toward developing] personal confidence, courage and the will to act" (p. 34). Another crucial aspect of culturally relevant teaching, in addition to centering the cultural knowledges of students of color, is to support teachers and students in identifying the oppressive power structures that maintain whiteness as dominant, as well as to make visible racism as structure (Aronson & Laughter, 2016). This teaching paradigm also emphasizes teachers' critical reflection on issues of inequity. In doing so, CRP presents an intentional way for teachers of color to reject and deny marginalizing messages of "otherness" through teaching for social justice as well as for white teachers to critically interrogate whiteness and racism as structure.

Research on race and education in the 1980s acknowledged the need for a collective phrase and approach to pedagogy beyond normalized, white, and middle-class conceptions of teaching and learning. In this vein, Ladson-Billings' (1995) ideas for how to approach teaching by centering the cultural knowledge of students of color, termed "culturally relevant pedagogy," has since entered the lexicon of mainstream education (Paris, 2012). Ladson-Billings (2001) outlined the three central tenets of CRP: (1) academic success; (2) cultural competence; and (3) sociopolitical consciousness. Academic success means teachers must establish clearly defined achievement goals, believe in the potential for achievement for *all* students, and operate under the assumption that knowledge is produced, not reproduced, between teachers and students. Additionally, teachers who take up the idea of academic success under CRP reject the deficit discourse frequently imposed upon diverse student bodies, or the belief that students of color are at an inherent deficit in contrast to their white student counterparts. The second tenet, cultural competency, means investing in the cultures of communities of color as the basis for learning in ways that are meaningful and relevant for teachers and students together. This tenet promotes the respect for and validation of a variety of cultural practices and values reflective of the outside lives of school community members, and cultivates an understanding of the way cultural backgrounds serve to define and construct identity. Finally, a sociopolitical consciousness means teachers must recognize how the situated knowledge generated in schools is located within broader social contexts, incorporate elements of social justice into curricula across disciplines, and work toward changing inequities that divide social groups among "racial, ethnic, cultural, linguistic and class lines" (Ladson-Billings, 2001, p. 104).

The impact of Ladson-Billings' (1995) introduction of the ideas of CRP to the greater educational community has been long lasting and wide ranging, resulting in an entire multipronged subsection of educational literature devoted to the topic. Some scholars have examined successful and affirming pedagogical practices and conceptions of teaching that engage with notions of CRP. For example, Lipman (1995) made the case for teachers who engage in CRP as a crucial missing element in fostering academic success for students of color, particularly as schools continue the trend of de facto segregation. Milner (2011) and Powell (1997) explored the significant and positive impact of white teachers who aimed to develop cultural congruency with their students of color by building out their own cultural competencies within their classrooms, strengthening relationships with students, and implementing a collective approach by inviting students to learn together. Gay and Kirkland (2003) and Howard (2003) both identified specific practices in teacher education programs that hinder preservice teachers' progress toward valuing and understanding CRP, such as the focus on technical mastery without critical reflexivity. Gay and Kirkland (2003) and Howard (2003) also both argued that preservice teachers need to be explicitly taught how to engage in critical reflection, along with modeling, practicing, and applying pedagogies related to critical consciousness. Further, Borrero, Flores, and de la Cruz (2016) illustrated how enacting CRP for new teachers of color is a way to self-affirm their own power in the face of marginalization from the profession by working and "giving back" within urban public schools.

Another theme in the literature on CRP is the examination of the pedagogical ways in which teachers can "honor [the] multiple voices and cultural practices" of children of color (Souto-Manning & Mitchell, 2010, p. 275). Dutro, Kazemi, Balf, and Lin (2008) argue that the complexities of teacher praxis when engaging or attempting to engage in CRP "bump up" against children's understanding of themselves in crucial ways, serving as a reminder of the importance of student-centered pedagogies within this epistemological approach to teaching. Likewise, Friend and Caruthers (2015) illustrated, from a CRP perspective, the role that autonomy and agency should play in approaches to teaching alongside the school reform agenda. A third theme within CRP literature and research focuses on challenging the norms and assumptions of teachers' notions of multiculturalism and approaches to teaching students of color. Cochran-Smith (1995) decried the "safe" approaches to multiculturalism (e.g., "basket making" as cultural practice) often utilized by teachers in favor of more direct means of addressing inequity across cultural and socioeconomic markers, thus promoting the idea of developing teachers' sociopolitical consciousness. Young (2010) determined that white teachers' implicit cultural biases, along with the nature of structural racism within school settings, prevented teachers from implementing CRP in their classrooms. Allen, Jackson and Knight (2012) "pushed back" against conceptions of African immigrant youth as unable to be successful in the classroom and instead called for teachers to enact CRP within curricula in order to reposition diverse student bodies as assets. The examples cited here are just a small snippet of the research that has emerged from a lens of CRP in the last 30+ years. These studies, as well as a multitude of others, provide a wealth of information on the potential impact of utilizing CRP and the meaning-making teachers and students might cultivate through this approach to pedagogy.

Yet, in spite of the widespread acceptance and general exaltation of CRP, and a significant body of research to support the three tenets, it still remains difficult to wholly and fully implement with the original intentions as described by Ladson-Billings (1995). There is a growing amount of educational literature problematizing the lack of social justice pedagogies, curricula, and policies enacted by teachers, schools, districts, and teacher education programs (McCarty & Lee, 2014; Paris & Alim, 2012). Much of the research and recommendations on this topic explore how little more than the bare minimum attention is given to critical perspectives, indicating that social justice as praxis is still a difficult pedagogical endeavor. Ladson-Billings herself, in an article (2014) revisiting her landmark term, described how few teachers "rarely push students to consider critical perspectives on policies and practices that may have direct impact on their lives and communities" (p. 78). Instead, teachers, teacher educators, and administrators often choose to soften the directness of the third tenet, sociopolitical consciousness. By focusing on the first two, successful academic achievements and the celebration of cultural practices, the pedagogies of CRP are more palatable for whites within educational communities. This circling or avoidance of a direct confrontation with the social and historical inequity of schooling means that even teachers with foundational knowledge on CRP, who are able to explicitly acknowledge how cultural capital is unrecognized within school contexts, avoid presenting a critical perspective on systematic inequality in classrooms. This represents one of the ways whiteness hinders an understanding of equity; white teachers often retreat into the safety of generic "multiculturalism," celebrating diversity without acknowledging the historical or policy-based inequality framing the context of modern school communities.

The Problems of "Multiculturalism" in Teacher Education Programs

In order to better prepare teachers who can capably take up all three tenets of CRP in the classroom, literature in the field has established teacher education programs as a crucial component of the processes by which future teachers come to understand and feel confident in enacting CRP. Teacher education programs are the key linchpin in the teacher pipeline, meaning that this is a critical time period in a teacher's occupational socialization into the profession to introduce, model, and explore the fundamentals of this teaching approach. Many teacher education programs are ineffective in developing future teachers who are knowledgeable of social justice pedagogies and willing to work to destabilize discourses of colorblindness, meritocracy, and white interest convergence often embedded within school policies, curricula, and pedagogies. For example, Fitchett, Starker, and Salyers (2012) found that preservice teachers who experienced curricula and pedagogies of CRP had increased rates of self-efficacy in their own ability to engage in these practices when they became full-fledged teachers, thus demonstrating the importance of embedding CRP throughout the duration of preservice teachers' time at their teacher education programs.

Not only do many teacher education programs devalue the insights and emotions of their often-marginalized preservice teachers of color, they also do not usually provide much guidance on antiracist or social justice pedagogies or attempt to disrupt whiteness as centered and racism as structure (Kohli, 2009). It is not uncommon for this topic to be bracketed off as its own single course, typically coded in "safe" terms such as "Multicultural Education" or "Teaching for Diversity," instead of being interwoven throughout an entire sequence within a teacher training program (Hytten & Warren, 2003). In order to address some of these problematic takes on teaching multicultural education, CRP rejects the multicultural education courses in many teacher education programs, often imbued with notions of colorblindness and meritocracy. This approach results in an "othering" of the ideas of culturally relevant and responsive pedagogy, as well as a noticeable lack of critical reflexivity and acknowledgment of how whiteness is centered within these programs by preservice teachers (Gay, 2010). Thus, adopting CRP as a framework when designing comprehensive teacher education programs can be helpful in destabilizing the generic understandings and representations of multicultural education within these programs that often promotes either a deficit discourse regarding students of color, a white savior complex, and/or teaching "beyond race" (Matias, 2013a,c).

There are two major problems with the traditional ways of addressing racism in teacher education through a lens of "multiculturalism." First, by relegating these ideas to their own individual course, the implicit message to preservice teachers is that antiracist or social justice pedagogies are separate from "regular" pedagogies and only something that need to be addressed for the duration of the single course. Second, the names and foci of these courses are intended to keep white preservice teachers comfortable in their complicity with whiteness by using "neutral" or "soft" terms such as "multiculturalism." The content of "multicultural education" courses rarely names or addresses the damaging discourses of colorblindness, meritocracy, and white interest convergence, deflecting fundamental issues of racism within education that have led individual programs, departments, colleges, and accreditation bodies to require such a course in the first place (Gay, 2010; Ladson-Billings, 2001). These types of singular courses often locate a marginalized position within preservice teacher education programs, and may be viewed by students as an additional requirement or simply another course to get through rather than as a, or possibly *the*, fundamental component to their overall teacher education and socialization. In short, social justice or antiracist approaches to teacher education do not currently occupy the centered position within preservice teacher preparation programs that they should in order to be effective.

A CRP teaching paradigm applied within educational disciplines means that there should not be a distinction between the "regular" pedagogy courses and the "multicultural" pedagogy course. Instead, antiracist and CRP should be centralized within all teacher training program pedagogies, regardless if teachers intend to work in predominantly white schools or in schools with a high population of students of color. Yet, in spite of this rallying call by scholars and educators alike, most teacher education programs continuously maintain a separation between the idea of "multicultural" education and general pedagogy courses, instead of embedding CRP within and across all the methods and content courses that are required for preservice teachers. The fact that many of these programs have not changed their requirements and program design in spite of the overwhelming indications from research on the topic that, given rapidly shifting student demographics, it is necessary for *all* future teachers to be culturally responsive educators, is an example of white interest convergence. Ultimately, most teacher training programs fail to cultivate students' critical consciousness and critical emotional literacies about racism as structure in the United States, and end up reproducing the existing cycle of white teacher socialization. In doing so, white teachers experience superficial courses on multicultural education but rarely actually challenge or disrupt coded displays of whiteness and continued white pedagogies (Sleeter, 2017). Taking up a CRP approach to teacher education means disavowing traditional conceptions of "multicultural" education and instead, through pedagogical praxis and a paradigmatic shift, deconstructing notions of whiteness that maintain white dominance and subsequent subordination of people of color within teacher training programs.

Culturally Sustaining Pedagogies

Since its inception more than two decades ago, while CRP is today widely "accepted" (although rarely enacted) within schools and teacher education programs, recent literature has grappled with the limitations of CRP, aiming to expand its application in ways which are both more meaningful and more useful in the context of racial diversity within public school education in the United States (Lee & Walsh, 2017; McCarty & Lee, 2014; Paris, 2012; Paris & Alim, 2017). For instance, Paris (2012) suggested the call to reinterpret CRP based on the idea that the terms "responsive" or "relevant" are not specific or useful enough to truly support the lived experiences of teachers of color. Paris (2012) argued that these terms are analogous to the word "tolerance" in multicultural education, fraught with ambivalence, and continue the social order of whiteness as dominant by implicitly promoting a neoliberal "equality for all" mantra. Additionally, he wrote that the use of the terms "responsive" (Gay, 2010) or "relevant" do not "explicitly enough support the linguistic and cultural dexterity and plurality necessary for success and access" (Paris, 2012, p. 95) for teachers and students of color within the educational system of the United States. Specifically, Paris (2012) called for an expansion of the concept of CRP on the basis that the implications of the commonly used terms "relevance" and "responsiveness" do not ensure that the heritages, cultures, customs and values of historically oppressed communities will be accurately presented, valued, and legitimated in schools.

In an effort to revitalize a framework often misinterpreted within academic and educational circles, Paris (2012) offered up the term "culturally sustaining pedagogy" (CSP) in lieu of CRP. From a teaching perspective, CSP provides *all* teachers, teachers of color and white teachers, a means of maintaining and supporting their own cultural competencies as well as that of their students while concurrently teaching within dominant cultural norms. This re-envisioning of CRP facilitates both "within-group cultural practices" and "common, across-group cultural practices" for students and teachers of color to not only exist but also thrive and be both sustained and sustaining (Paris, 2012, p. 95). As this new imagining of the original framework has gained traction, some scholars have moved beyond CRP toward more encompassing notions of multicultural education. For example, McCarty & Lee (2014) examined the potential for reconceptualizing CRP as culturally relevant *and* sustaining practice within Native American educational communities. The authors illustrated how teachers can provide access to academic achievement through linguistic work by focusing on both indigenous and English language learning while simultaneously critiquing the colonizing pedagogies that "reduce the multidimensionality of human experience" (p. 118) to singular standards supported by whiteness. Lee and Walsh (2017) utilized the tenets of CSP in order to develop a youth participatory action research project in the hopes of cultivating teacher pedagogies that support the developing identities and cultural fluidity of students of color, along with a space for minoritized school community members to analyze their own experiences through a critical lens. Such examples illustrate the potential for CSP to be a pedagogy of transformation, toward new and critical understandings of how school communities, educational policies, and pedagogy scholarship might shift away from dominant white, Eurocentric ideologies.

Another component of CSP is a call to move toward a critical perspective, emphasizing the tenet of CRP most-often passed or glossed over, even by educators who try to enact CRP in their classrooms. CSP aims to disrupt the hierarchical hegemony of whiteness dominating education under a "panoptic 'White gaze'" that devalues and delegitimizes the "linguistic, literate, and cultural practices" of communities of color (Paris & Alim, 2014, p. 86), shedding light on racialized discourses that position teachers and students of color as "less than" their white counterparts. Although one of the goals of CRP is to raise and develop a sociopolitical consciousness among teachers, administrators, and students, critical pedagogy plays a far more central role in CSP. First, critiquing imbalanced power relations within societal structures through critical pedagogical practices is one subsection of a critical perspective embraced by CSP. Second, Paris & Alim (2014) argue that CSP scholars and practitioners must also turn the critical gaze "inward." This means finding time and space, as well as providing the means, for pedagogies that not only celebrate and promote cultural knowledge but also identify the oppressive undercurrents within some of these various cultural knowledges. For example, teachers might use Hip Hop music as a learning tool within progressive or liberating CSP pedagogies, but unless coupled with an examination of the undercurrent of misogyny and homophobia at times apparent within this musical genre, these intersecting harmful messages remain unchecked, untroubled, and normalized within Hip Hop culture (Mcarty & Lee, 2014; Paris & Alim, 2017). A CSP approach to using Hip Hop as pedagogy means that not only would this medium of communication be included as a way to engage students in the learning objectives for the particular unit or class but would also facilitate students' sociopolitical critique of the genre itself as well as the social constructs Hip Hop often addresses, such as the power or oppression of people of color.

From an inward critique to an outward gaze, CRP and CSP aim to move toward notions of intersectionality, or a recognition of and appreciation for "global identities" beyond any one single racial, ethnic, or cultural group (Ladson-Billings, 2014, p. 82). Intersectionality recognizes that the multiple, complex, layered, and nuanced identities of an individual may result in power differentials between and among groups due to systematic or structural inequity (Gillborn, 2015). What this means is that no individual is reduced to a unitary social identifier but rather is an amalgam of constructs, from which a person shifts in and out of, depending on context, desire, and assigned identified meanings. While CRP and CSP were, first and foremost, developed as direct reactions to racial inequity, one of the vital tenets of this reframing is to move away from singular, over-simplified, or assumed unilateral heritages and practices of communities of color (Paris & Alim, 2014). From this position, it is therefore important to recognize the multiple marginalized positions of teachers of color, how these multiple and shifting positions might impact their meaning-making within school, *and* how cultural resources might evolve as meaningful for a vast array of historically marginalized communities of color (Paris & Alim, 2017).

Culturally Disrupting Pedagogies and Beyond

Whiteness is embedded within education to the point where it is difficult to see and name, thus necessitating a shift in pedagogy towards both CRP and

CSP as means of destabilizing white supremacy within various educational contexts (e.g., elementary, secondary, postsecondary, and academia) while simultaneously supporting teachers of color located in these predominantly white frameworks of education and educational success. A rise in neoliberal approaches to pedagogies, as well as standardized curricula, also indicates that culturally relevant and sustaining education continues to be marginalized within broad educational discourse (Aronson & Laughter, 2016). Milner's (2017) recent review of literature on the implementation of CRP found that race was often lacking as the central element within supposedly culturally relevant attempts at teaching, or was addressed only superficially. As CRP has been widened, stretched, reframed, and reconstructed, some of its original meanings about the centering of racial inequality have been lost (Milner, 2017). While the majority of research, theory, and practice has focused on both CRP and CSP as means of working for academic success for students of color, it is possible that these pedagogical strategies need to be revised, given the rising rates of school segregation. That is, the frameworks of CRP and CSP are not necessarily appropriate in predominantly white schools where teachers can center whiteness and utilize their white privilege to maintain colorblind perspectives imbued with notions of meritocracy.

San Pedro (2018) begins to dissect this issue by offering up the idea of culturally *disrupting* pedagogy (CDP), or a way of "creating ruptures in schooling and social systems that counter the normalizing of whiteness" (p. 1221) and make visible hegemonic power imbalances. While the disruption of whiteness is an inherent or implicit component of CRP and CSP, these theories of pedagogy are rightfully intended to center the experiences and knowledges of historically marginalized communities of color. This is in contrast to assisting white teachers and students in realizing their participation in an unbalanced, historically oppressive, and often invisible system of white supremacy. It is evident based on the information presented in this chapter that *all* of these pedagogies are needed within schools and teacher education programs but are context driven and must be utilized strategically in order to revitalize the teacher pipeline toward schools and learning experiences that encompass and embrace a diversity of identities and experiences.

In order to destabilize whiteness within education, teachers, scholars, and teacher educators have developed and studied culturally sustaining and/or CRP as potentially impactful on uprooting racist, white-based pedagogies, curricula, and assessments *if* they include a focus on cultivating sociopolitical consciousness. Aronson and Laughter's (2016) synthesis of a large body of literature on the topic of CRP concluded that teachers and teacher education programs were crucial in facilitating broader and stronger enactments of this pedagogy, mostly because it was done by teachers who believed deeply and righteously that this was a way to make social change. Critical pedagogies that facilitate growing awareness of structural inequity within education related to imbalanced racialized hierarchies, along with a multitude of other intersecting marginalizing social identifiers, need to be implemented both in teacher education programs for preservice teachers and in K-12 classroom settings in schools across the United States.

Continuing the Conversation about "Race Talk": CRP to Cultivate Empowerment for Teachers

A culturally relevant, sustaining, and/or disrupting framework for teaching can be useful to empower both teachers of color and white teachers and preservice teachers, building resistance "from the margins" and allowing scholars and educators to enact their own understanding of critical consciousness and sustain a social justice-oriented curriculum. The core ideas of CRP/CSP stem from critical race theory (CRT), prioritizing the notion of social transformation and/or working toward an epistemological viewpoint shift within and among social groups (Modica, 2015; Solórzano, Ceja, & Yosso, 2000). In fact, the idea of social revolution has underscored much of the political and social justice work by teachers and activists of color in various fights for social change during the course of the history of the United States (Bonilla-Silva, 2015). If CRT aims to address racialized power imbalances within America, consistently preserving white supremacy as the ultimate power holder, then one critical intention of this theory and, therefore, CRP and CSP, is to change flawed power dynamics toward more equitable constructions of whiteness, race, and minoritization, both individually and structurally (Jennings & Lynn, 2005). This is important not only for potentially marginalized teachers and preservice teachers of color but also for white teachers and preservice teachers, who, without formal training, may lack the language dexterity, critical understandings, and the desire for social transformation necessary to engage in CRP and CSP.

The foundation of social transformation towards agency, empowerment, and critical resistance are particularly salient within educational settings. While critical race scholars have identified schools and education as sites of social reproduction, they can also be sites of contestation as minoritized teachers enact agency in order to attempt to resist the reproduction of dominance discourses of whiteness (Allen, 2015). For example, Baez (2000) examined how faculty of color at predominantly white institutions of higher education reconceptualized notions of service within academia toward a critical agency by working for community, political, or personal goals for social change. Rodriguez (2011) described how engaging in acts of co-storytelling with her Latina female student-teacher research participants encouraged both the author and students to redefine their identities from marginalized to empowered through acts of transformation and resistance. The idea of implementing critical pedagogies from a CRP lens illustrates how a classroom can be a space where students and educators challenge hegemonic norms and resist traditional learning or assigned meanings that devalue cultural knowledge within their educational microcontexts (Smith-Maddox & Solórzano, 2002). Case in point, Kim (2001) cultivated her minoritized students' agency through the pedagogies they co-created within her classroom setting by aiming to help students reflect on and resist dominant racialized discourses. Berry (2005, 2010) enacted personal agency toward a critical praxis within her own pedagogies as a teacher educator of color, exploring how engaged pedagogies fit within culturally relevant and critical race frameworks. By resisting institutionalized racial hierarchies, teachers and administrators of color are then able to redefine what holds value and meaning for them within school contexts, and how to amplify and legitimize these new conceptualizations of what knowledge is most valuable in such a way as to destabilize privileged white and Eurocentric forms of knowledge.

Sustaining, centralizing, and legitimating the cultural knowledge of communities of color toward a sense of agency in the educational process has been determined to result in successfully educating underserved and underappreciated students of color, who are frequently concentrated in socioeconomically oppressed communities (Allen, 2015; Brown & Davis, 2001; Morris, 2004). While this is something that many teachers of color have historically been able to recognize on an individual level, it is only in the past few decades that scholarship on the topic has begun to identify the long-term impact of enacting CRP on *teachers'* experiences. In particular, researchers have started to explore how these pedagogies might foster a heightened sense of self and a greater sense of purpose for teachers of color (Allen, 2015; Foster, 1997; Morris, 2004). Foster (1997) explored the life histories of Black teachers, many of whom lived and taught through the *Brown vs. Board of Education* ruling of 1954, and how they were sustained through times of racial tension and scrutiny by enacting CRP. Morris (2004) examined the empowering pedagogies used by two predominantly Black schools as places where Black teachers could feel comfortable and confident in their profession. Morris (2004) concluded that strategies such as intergenerational bonding among school community members, building trust and a rapport with parents by actively reaching out and welcoming them in, and affirming students' cultural values by creating a school environment where students could "see themselves and their culture within the schooling process" (p. 93), all worked to create a "successful" (as measured by student test performances) educational community. Allen (2015) identified the strategies teachers employed in order to successfully engage their students of color, such as holding students to high standards and accountable for their learning, thereby disrupting deficit discourses about urban schools and students of color, along with establishing teacher agency by advocating for students of color and challenging students' self-defeating resistance to academic success. Brown and Davis (2001) identified historically Black colleges and universities (HBCU), in which some teacher training programs are located, as important and agentic spaces for students of color. HBCUs offer opportunities for social capital to be produced through the distribution of resources and knowledge, serving as a social equalizer by generating access to education for students of color in a climate that values them. Agency and empowerment are thus crucial social justice tools in addressing racism within education and it is clear from existing literature that CRP can be effective at cultivating these characteristics within appropriate school settings.

CONCLUSION

The narratives of the Black, Latina, and Asian female teachers in this book highlight the importance of identifying how those located within oppressive contexts can draw strength from their position of marginality and be "empowered by their sense of belonging to a group whose very survival has been dependent upon the collective ability to resist" (Ward, 1996, p. 97). It is vital for educational research and scholarship on race and racial injustice to present the potential for critical resilience within oppressive school contexts for teachers of color. Schools frequently maintain structural racialized oppression toward teachers of color but the teachers' counterstories in this book serve as an important reminder that the retelling of their stories should not be framed within tropes of victimhood and subjection, particularly if the work is coming from white teachers, scholars, professors, and researchers engaged in topics of diversity, racism, and multiculturalism. Rather than operate from a "deficit" or "savior" position and maintain a hold on whiteness as dominant, it is imperative that educators and scholars committed to enacting CRP and CSP in schools employ an agentic perspective, recognizing the autonomy of individuals in reframing their experiences toward empowerment and validation. In other words, the agency and critical emotional literacies of "othered" teachers should be centered within a deeper understanding of schools as sites of oppression. This approach to understanding the lives and experiences of teachers of color facilitates the broader aim of antiracist scholars and educators to destabilize discourses of whiteness and invisible yet pervasive forms of racism embedded within the education system in the United States, moving instead toward expansive pedagogies which are culturally relevant, sustaining, and disrupting (McLaren, 1998; Tejeda, Espinoza, & Gutierrez, 2003).

Adopting a "communities of color" epistemology that locates minoritized communities' emotional and cultural knowledge as central products of an unjust and inherently and structurally racist state is a direct reflection of the ideas of CRP (Matias & Mackey, 2016). By taking up this epistemology, the emotions of teachers of color in terms of "feeling" and "living" race, along with a commitment to social justice teaching, are legitimated as valid and valuable pedagogical stances. As such, the fundamentals of CRP and CSP have the potential to disrupt the dominant norms of whiteness within both the education system and the teacher pipeline by developing students' and preservice teachers' sociopolitical or critical consciousness. This is the key component to enacting culturally relevant and sustaining pedagogies which would allow the politics of racialized emotions to be acknowledged and destabilized as forms of white supremacy. It is through the development of a critical consciousness within pedagogical praxis that teachers of color may reconcile their own strong feelings regarding race-based discrimination and prejudice within a framework of agency, thus affording marginalized teachers a way to reposition themselves as both empowered and powerful.

While the integration of a social justice agenda in schools is an urgent enterprise, one of the barriers to enacting culturally relevant, sustaining, and/or disrupting pedagogies in schools is the strong emotional responses tied up in "race work." "Race work" is difficult for white teachers and can be particularly difficult for teachers of color who must consistently negotiate whiteness within their professional teacher identity contexts (Jay, 2009). Emotionality is worth exploring in more depth in order to ground notions of CRP and CSP within the potential for providing teachers of color with agency and pride in their sense of selves as educators, especially related to enacting social justice pedagogies and working for social change within their school contexts. Additionally, emotionality can assist white teachers in unpacking and self-critiquing their own complicated emotions regarding invisible racism and white privilege. Teaching is an emotional act of identity, in spite of professional discourse discouraging emotional attachments and expression (Durden, Dooley, & Truscott, 2014; Malin, 2000). Ahmed (2001) describes emotions as circulating between "signifiers" of difference in relationships that "align individuals with communities, or bodily space with social space" (p. 11). Yet these emotions can also serve to "misalign" individuals if the emotions do not match the expected norms and values of a collective body. The predication toward emotional attachments and associations within teaching suggests that teachers of color in predominantly white schools may be "othered" because of their strong emotional responses to whiteness and racism, and thus need to engage in significant mental and psychological "work" due to their misaligned and/or repressed emotional state of being. On the other side, white teachers' "misalignment" of emotions reflects long-standing or historical detachment from issues of racial inequity and deep-rooted fears, insecurities, anxieties, and lack of language mastery on how to address their own sense of self as white.

The repression and control of teachers' emotions in schools result in a politic of emotion, preventing teachers of color from expressing the pain and hurt of racism and instead, requiring them to maintain a façade of polite acceptance to norms of whiteness (Ahmed, 2009). Even white teachers who desire or intend to speak up about issues of racial injustice and oppression are silenced by a politic of emotion, which prevents the social acceptance of strong or overt emotions regarding "race work." When teachers of color express negative emotions such as anger, fear, frustration, or sadness, white teachers and administrators often dismiss or reject these expressions as "unreasonable" or "out of control," positioning teachers of color as highly emotional, charged, unstable, and unable to be met with reason and logic. A politic of emotion ultimately psychologizes emotional responses as something that stems internally, rather than being the product of the contextual or collective social forces within which a teacher is located (Ahmed, 2004a). Thus, a politic of emotion represents a neoliberal approach to maintaining whiteness and racial hierarchies as teachers of color who ultimately do express strong emotional responses are deemed responsible for their own emotions (and therefore lacking control over these emotions), rather than understood as reacting to racism as an external stimuli worthy of an emotional response (Durden et al., 2014). In contrast, white teachers' emotions about racism (e.g., white tears, white pity, white righteousness) are accepted and included within the social and cultural collective order of schools. A stronghold of white emotions within social institutions such as schools means that doing "diversity work" becomes about "changing perceptions of whiteness rather than changing the whiteness" of the institution itself (Ahmed, 2009, p. 45). This maintains a paradox within white schools where diversity work is given "lip service" but real change toward upheaving whiteness as dominant is never fully acted upon. As such, teachers of color must consistently perform the additional constraining emotional labor of working to "maintain control" over their emotions in order to fit in within white school environments.

While emotionality is often employed to analyze the negative emotional responses stemming from structural inequity, such as invisible racism and dominant whiteness within education, emotionality can also be used to understand emotions as mobilizing and uplifting. Ahmed (2004b) writes that "emotions are what move us. But emotions are also about attachments, what connects us . . . What moves us, what makes us feel, is also that which holds us in place, or gives us a dwelling" (p. 27). Thus, minoritized or marginalized teachers' connections and sentiments of value for their work, particularly when focused on enacting social change within their oppressive school contexts, can be understood as a form of emotional attachment, both validating and affirming. If feelings of self-worth and self-affirmation are understood as "truths," or what teachers of color know, believe, and are working toward, then emotional truths associated with making a difference in their schools and in their students' lives serve to both outweigh and validate the pain of living, working, and existing as a racialized entity within pre- dominantly white spaces (Matias, 2013a). Emotionality can also be a useful approach to understanding, deconstructing, and destabilizing white teachers' responses when confronted with issues of racism, white privilege, and white dominance within pedagogy, curricula, and policies as a way to critique and reframe white emotions about race rather than accept them. CRP and CSP are ways of teaching which should be enacted by *all* teachers—teachers of color and white teachers, and therefore, it is essential that white emotionality about race and racism is a part of these pedagogies in order to provide white teachers with stronger reflective praxis regarding their own white positionali- ties and identities.

Applying a lens of emotionality to educational contexts to analyze the experiences of teachers of color provides strong support for the need for greater enactment of culturally relevant, sustaining, and disrupting pedago- gies that recognize emotions as critical in developing an empowered sense of self, or critical emotional literacy (O'Connor, 2008; Osgood, 2010; Winans, 2012). Culturally relevant, sustaining, and disrupting pedagogies to cultivate critical emotional literacy are crucial for helping white teachers develop criti- cal consciousness, who may never have been challenged to address their own white privilege or may feel anxious or unsure of strategies and language for initiating social justice pedagogies. These pedagogies are also particularly relevant for teachers of color, given the nature of the racialized repression of emotions they might endure. Additionally, developing critical emotional literacy among white teachers and teacher candidates can provide a means of decoding white emotions of anger, guilt, and defensiveness when confronted with their own indicators of whiteness and racism (Matias & Mackey, 2016). For example, Matias and Mackey (2016) aimed to develop pedagogies of critical emotional literacy within their mostly white and female teacher can- didates through emotional investment, a sharing of emotional burdens, and developing a vision of humanity that communicates a loving environment, as opposed to a colorblind coopting environment. By developing a pedagogy for understanding how a politic of emotion maintains racial power imbalances within social institutions such as schools, teachers of color can reframe their strong emotions regarding racism and discrimination toward empowerment and self-affirmation.

The experiences of the emotionality of whiteness that Mara shared in this chapter showed the potential depth and breadth of feelings related to "feeling race." As a white person, Mara could avoid "feeling race," as she had most of her life, until directly confronted with the implications of this avoidance through both the racialized pain of people of color and her own white pain related to white privilege and invisible racism. The incidences she described in the beginning of the chapter—the devastation of the probationary charge against her colleague, a teacher of color, for the ways she communicated with her students, along with the overtly racist taunts of her white daughter toward a fellow Black student, both accompanied by deep emotional turmoil on Mara's part—served as a catalyst for Mara to grapple with the emotional fallout of coming face-to-face with "feeling race." Mara's internal reflexivity contextualized within a span of scholarly and theoretical knowledge of culturally relevant, sustaining, and disrupting pedagogies afforded her a way to develop self-acceptance around the paradoxical idea of embodying whiteness while simultaneously critiquing whiteness. This reflection and acceptance has resulted in more meaningful pedagogies within her professional praxis, directly addressing issues of whiteness in education without fear and with a clear and persuasive voice. As Mara evolved in her understandings of "feeling race," she became more willing to present these ideas within her classrooms as a teacher educator and to develop her preservice teachers' understandings of culturally relevant, sustaining, and disrupting pedagogies. This reconciliation of Mara's emotional ties to internalized whiteness with her personal commitment to racial equity and social justice illustrate the potential of emotionality within approaches to pedagogy which are directly intended to foster a critical consciousness among both students and teachers. Taken together, the stories and "small teaching episodes" of the teachers of color, along with Mara's personal narratives as a teacher, teacher educator, and motherscholar, present a compelling argument for the need for enacting culturally relevant, sustaining, and disrupting pedagogies from a lens of emotionality in order to destabilize dominant norms of whiteness within education. In doing so, another vision of school emerges, one in which issues of social justice are centered through critical pedagogies, interrogating whiteness and cultivating the beauty, joy, and love of "feeling race"—where whiteness as an ideology is de-centered while simultaneously celebrating, valuing, and legitimating a multitude of identities, ethnicities, and cultures.

Bibliography

Ahmed, S. (2001). Communities that feel: Intensity, difference, and attachment. In A. Koivunen, & S. Paasonen (eds), *Affective Encounters: Rethinking Embodiment in Feminist Media Studies Conference* (pp. 10–24). Turku, Finland: University of Turku.

Ahmed, S. (2004a). Declarations of whiteness: The non-performativity of anti-racism racism. *borderlands*, *3*(2), 1–15.

Ahmed, S. (2004b). Collective feelings: Or, the impression left by others. *Theory, Culture and Society*, *21*(2), 25–42.

Ahmed, S. (2009). Embodying diversity: Problems and paradoxes for black feminists. *Race Ethnicity and Education*, *12*(1), 41–52.

Allen, K.M., Jackson, I., & Knight, M. (2012). Complicating culturally relevant pedagogy: Unpacking West African immigrants' cultural identities. *International Journal of Multicultural Education*, *14*(2), 1–27.

Allen, Q. (2015). Race, culture, and agency: Examining the ideologies and practices of U.S. teachers of Black male students. *Teaching and Teacher Education*, *47*, 71–81.

Allen, R.L. (2014). Whiteness and critical pedagogy. *Educational Philosophy and Theory*, *36*(2), 121–136.

Allen, R.L., & Liou, D. (2019). Managing whiteness: The call for educational leadership to breach the contractual expectations of white supremacy. *Urban Education*, *54*(5), 677–705.

Amos, Y.T. (2016). Voices of teacher candidates of color on white race evasion: 'I worried about my safety!' *International Journal of Qualitative Studies in Education*, *29*(8), 1002–1015.

Andrews, K.T. (2002). Movement-countermovement dynamics and the emergence of new institutions: The case of "white flight" schools in Mississippi. *Social Forces*, *80*(3), 911–936.

Arnesen, E. (2001). Whiteness and the historians' imagination. *International Labor and Working-Class History*, *60*, 3–32.

Arnez, N. (1978). Implementation of desegregation as a discriminatory process. *Journal of Negro Education, 47*(1), 28–45.

Aronson, B., & Laughter, J. (2016). The theory and practice of culturally relevant education: A synthesis of research across content areas. *Review of Educational Research, 86*(1), 163–206.

Azzarito, L. (2009). The panopticon of physical education: Pretty, active and ideally white. *Physical Education and Sport Pedagogy, 14*(1), 19–39.

Baez, B. (2000). Race-related service and faculty of color: Conceptualizing critical agency in academe. *Higher Education, 39*(3), 363–391.

Baszile, D.T. (2008a). The oppressor within: A counterstory of race, repression and teacher reflection. *Urban Review, 40*(4), 371–385.

Baszile, D.T. (2008b). Beyond all reason indeed: The pedagogical promise of critical race testimony. *Race, Ethnicity and Education, 11*(3), 251–265.

Bell, D.A. (1979). *Bakke,* minority admissions, and the usual price of racial remedies. *California Law Review, 67*(1), 3–19.

Bell, D.A. (1980). *Brown v. Board of Education* and the interest-convergence dilemma. *Harvard Law Review, 93*(3), 518–534.

Bell, D.A. (1984). The hurdle too high: Class-based roadblocks to racial remediation. *Buffalo Law Review, 33*(1), 1–34.

Bell, D.A. (2004). *Silent covenants: Brown v. Board of Education and the unfulfilled hopes for racial reform.* Oxford, UK: Oxford Press.

Bennett, C., McWhorter, L., & Kuykendall, J. (2006). "Will I ever teach?": Latino and African American students' perceptions on PRAXIS I. *American Educational Research Journal, 43*(3), 531–575.

Bernal, D.R., Burciaga, R., & Carmona, J.F. (2012). Chicana/Latina *testimonios*: Mapping the methodological, pedagogical, and political. *Equity and Excellence in Education, 45*(3), 363–372.

Berry, T.R. (2005). Black on Black education: Personally engaged pedagogy for/by African American pre-service teachers. *The Urban Review, 37*(1), 31–48.

Berry, T.R. (2010). Engaged pedagogy and critical race feminism. *Educational Foundations, 24*, 19–26.

Boler, M., & Zembylas, M. (2003). Discomforting truths: Rethinking education for social change. In P. Trifonas (ed.), *Pedagogies of difference: Rethinking education for social change* (pp. 216–139). New York, NY: Routledge Falmer.

Bonilla-Silva, E. (2006). *Racism Without racists: Colorblind racism and the persistence of racial inequality in the United States.* Lanham, MD: Rowman & Littlefield.

Bonilla-Silva, E. (2015). The structure of racism in color-blind, "post racial" America. *American Behavioral Scientist, 59*(11), 1358–1376.

Bonilla-Silva, E., & Embrick, D. (2006). Racism without racists: "Killing me softly" with color blindness. In C.A. Rossatto, R.L. Allen, & M. Pruyan (eds), *Reinventing critical pedagogy: Widening the circle of anti-racist education* (pp. 21–34). Plymouth, UK: Rowman & Littlefield Publishers.

Borrero, N.E., Flores, E., & de la Cruz, G. (2016). Developing and enacting culturally relevant pedagogy: Voices of new teachers of color. *Equity and Excellence in Education, 49*(1), 27–40.

Boutte, G., & Jackson, T.O. (2014). Advice to white allies: Insights from faculty of color. *Race, Ethnicity and Education, 17*(5), 623–642.

Bowleg, L. (2008). When Black + lesbian + woman ≠ Black lesbian woman: The methodological challenges of qualitative and quantitative intersectionality research. *Sex Roles, 59*(5–6), 312–325.

Bowleg, L. (2012). The problem with the phrase women and minorities: Intersectionality: An important theoretical framework for public health. *American Journal of Public Health, 102*(7), 1267–1273.

Brickner, P., & Hanson, M. (2003). The American dreamer: Racial prejudices and discrimination as seen through the history of American immigration law. *Thomas Jefferson Law Review, 26*, 203–238.

Brodkin, K. (2002). *How the Jews became white folks and what that says about race in America.* New Brunswick, NJ: Rutgers University Press.

Brown, M.C., & Davis, J.E. (2001). The historically Black college as social contract, social capital, and social equalizer. *Peabody Journal of Education, 76* (1), 31–49.

Brunsma, D., Embrick, D., & Shin, J.H. (2017). Graduate students of color: Race, racism, and mentoring in the white waters of academia. *Sociology of Race and Ethnicity, 3*(1), 1–13.

Bryson, B. (2017). "They were constantly on the losing side of things": The pedagogical power of an African American teacher candidate bearing witness in teacher education. *Race, Ethnicity and Education, 20*(4), 527–545.

Cabrera, N.L. (2014). Exposing whiteness in higher education: White male college students minimizing racism, claiming victimization, and recreating white supremacy. *Race, Ethnicity and Education, 17*(1), 30–55.

Carter, D. (2008). Achievement as resistance: The development of a critical race achievement ideology among black achievers. *Harvard Educational Review, 78*(3), 466–497.

Carter, R. (1980). A reassessment of Brown v. Board. In D. Bell (ed.), *Shades of brown: New perspectives on school desegregation* (pp. 21–28). New York, NY: Teachers College Press.

Carter, R.T. (2007). Racism and psychological and emotional injury: Recognizing and assessing race-based traumatic stress. *The Counseling Psychologist, 35*(1), 13–105.

Cheruvu, R., Souto-Manning, M., Lencl, T., & Chin-Calubaquib, M. (2015). Race, isolation and exclusion: What early childhood educators need to know about the experiences of pre-service teachers of color. *The Urban Review, 47*(2), 237–265.

Clotfelter, C.T. (2001). Are whites still fleeing? Racial patterns and enrollment shifts in urban public schools, 1987–1996. *Journal of Policy Analysis and Management, 20*, 199–221.

Cochran-Smith, M. (1995). Colorblindness and basket making are not the answers: Confronting the dilemmas of race, culture, and language diversity in teacher education. *American Educational Research Journal, 32*(3), 493–522.

Cochran-Smith, M. (2010). Toward a theory of teacher education for social justice. In M. Fullan, A. Hargreaves, D. Hopkins, & A. Lieberman (eds), *The international handbook of educational change* (2nd edition, pp. 445–467). New York, NY: Springer Publishing.

Cole, B.A. (2009). Gender, narratives and intersectionality: Can personal experience approaches to research contribute to "undoing gender"? *International Review of Education, 55*(5–6), 561–578.

Convertino, C. (2016). Beyond ethnic tidbits: Toward a critical and dialogical model in multicultural social justice teacher preparation. *International Journal of Multicultural Education, 18*(2), 125–142.

Crenshaw, K.W. (1988). Race, reform, retrenchment: Transformation and legitimation in anti-discrimination law. *Harvard Law Review, 101*, 1331–1387.

Crenshaw, K.W. (1991). Mapping the margins: Intersectionality, identity politics, and violence against women of color. *Stanford Law Review, 43*, 1241–1299.

Davis, M., Vakalahi, H., & Scales, R. (2015). Women of color in the academy. In K. de Welde & A. Stepnick (eds), *The culture of silence: Confronting gender inequality and making change in higher education* (pp. 265–277). Sterling, VA: Stylus.

Delgado, R. (1987). The ethereal scholar: Does critical legal studies have what minorities want? *Harvard Civil Rights-Civil Liberties Law Review, 22*, 301–322.

Dingus, J.E. (2008). "I'm learning the trade": Mentoring networks of Black women teachers. *Urban Education, 43*(3), 361–377.

Dixson, A., Buras, K., & Jeffers, E. (2015). The color of reform: Race, education reform, and charter schools in post-Katrina New Orleans. *Qualitative Inquiry, 21*(3), 288–299.

Donahoo, S. (2006). Derailing desegregation: Legal efforts to end racial segregation in higher education before and after *Brown*. *Equity and Excellence in Education, 39*(4), 291–301.

Durden, T., Dooley, C.M., & Truscott, D. (2016). Race still matters: Preparing culturally relevant teachers. *Race, Ethnicity and Education, 19*(5), 1003–1024.

Dutro, E., Kazemi, E., Balf, R., & Lin, Y.S. (2008). "What are you and where are you from?" Race, identity, and the vicissitudes of cultural relevance. *Urban Education, 43*(3), 269–300.

Esposito, J. (2011). Negotiating the gaze and learning the hidden curriculum: A critical race analysis of the embodiment of female students of color at a predominantly white institution. *Journal for Critical Educational Policy Studies, 9*(2), 143–164.

Etheridge, S. (1979). Impact of the 1954 *Brown vs. Topeka Board of Education* decision on black educators. *Negro Educational Review, 30* (4), 217–232.

Evans-Winters, V., & Esposito, J. (2010). Other people's daughters: Critical race feminism and Black girls' education. *The Journal for Educational Foundations, 24*(1/2), 11–24.

Evans-Winters, V., & Hoff, P.T. (2011). The aesthetics of white racism in pre-service teacher education: A critical race theory perspective. *Race, Ethnicity and Education, 14*(4), 461–479.

Fairclough, A. (2004). The costs of Brown: Black teachers and school integration. *The Journal of American History, 91*(1), 43–55.

Farinde, A., Allen, A., & Lewis, C. (2016). Retaining Black teachers: An examination of Black female teachers' intentions to remain in K-12 classrooms. *Equity and Excellence in Education, 49*(1), 115–127.

Farinde, A., LeBlanc, J., & Otten, A. (2015). Pathways to teaching: An examination of Black females' pursuits of careers as K-12 teachers. *Educational Research Quarterly, 38*(3), 32–51.

Farinde-Wu, A., & Fitchett, P.G. (2018). Searching for satisfaction: Black female teachers' workplace climate and job satisfaction. *Urban Education, 53*(1), 86–112.

Finkelstein, M.J., Conley, V.M., & Schuster, J.H. (2016). *The faculty factor: Reassessing the American academy in a turbulent era.* Baltimore, MD: John Hopkins University Press.

Fitchett, P., Starker, T., & Salyers, B. (2012). Examining culturally responsive teaching self-efficacy in preservice social studies education course. *Urban Education, 47*(3), 585–611.

Foster, M. (1997). *Black teachers on teaching.* New York, NY: The New Press.

Franklin, V.P. (1990). "They rose and fell together": African American educators and community leadership, 1795–1954. *Journal of Education, 172*(3), 39–64.

Friend, J., & Caruthers, L. (2015). Transforming the school reform agenda: A framework for including student voice in urban school renewal. *Journal of Urban Learning, Teaching, and Research, 11,* 14–25.

Gallagher, C. (2016). Playing the white ethnic card: Using ethnic identity to deny contemporary racism. In A. Doane & E. Bonilla-Silva (eds), *White out: The continuing significance of racism* (pp. 145–159). London: Routledge.

Garte, R. (2017). American progressive education and the schooling of poor children: A brief history of a philosophy in practice. *International Journal of Progressive Education, 13*(2), 7–17.

Gay, G. (2004). Navigating marginality en route to the professoriate: Graduate students of color learning and living in academia. *International Journal of Qualitative Studies in Education, 17*(2), 265–288.

Gay, G. (2010). *Culturally responsive teaching: Theory, research and practice* (2nd edition). New York, NY: Teachers College Press.

Gay, G. (2013). Teaching to and through cultural diversity. *Curriculum Inquiry, 43*(1), 48–70.

Gay, G., & Kirkland, K. (2003). Developing cultural critical consciousness and self-reflection in preservice teacher education. *Theory into Practice, 42*(3), 181–187.

Gillborn, D. (2005). Education policy as an act of white supremacy: Whiteness, critical race theory and education reform. *Journal of Education Policy, 20*(4), 485–505.

Gillborn, D. (2006). Critical race theory and education: Racism and anti-racism in educational theory and praxis. *Discourse: Studies in the Cultural Politics of Education, 27*(1), 11–32.

Gillborn, D. (2012). The white working class, racism, and respectability: Victims, degenerates, and interest-convergence. In K. Bhopal & J. Preston (eds), *Intersectionality and race and education.* New York, NY: Routledge.

Gillborn, D. (2015). Intersectionality, critical race theory, and the primacy of racism, race, class, gender, and disability in education. *Qualitative Inquiry, 21*(3), 277–287.

Gillborn, D., & Ladson-Billings, G. (2010). Education and critical raced theory. In M. Apple, S.J. Ball, & L.A. Gandin (eds), *The Routledge international handbook of the sociology of education.* New York, NY: Routledge.

Giroux, H. (1983). Theories of reproduction and resistance in the new sociology of education: A critical analysis. *Harvard Educational Review*, *55*(3), 257–293.

Godfrey, P. (2008). The "other white": Mexican Americans and the impotency of whiteness in the segregation and desegregation of Texan public schools. *Urban Education, 41*(2), 247–261.

Goldhaber, D.R., & Hansen, M. (2010). Race, gender, and teacher testing: How informative a tool is teacher licensure testing? *American Educational Research Journal, 47*(1), 218–251.

Gomez, M., Rodriguez, T., & Agosto, V. (2008). Life histories of Latino/a teacher candidates. *Teachers College Record, 110*(8), 1639–1676.

Gonzalez, G. (2013). *Chicano education in the era of segregation.* Denton, TX: University of North Texas Press.

Grant, A., & Gillespie, L. (1993). *Joining the circle: A Practitioners' Guide to Responsive Education for Native Students.* Charleston, WV: (ERIC Clearinghouse on Rural Education and Small Schools No. ED 360 117).

Grant, C.A. (2004). Oppression, privilege, and high-stakes testing. *Multicultural perspectives, 6*(1), 3–11.

Hall, P.D. (2016). White fragility and affirmative action. *Journal of Race and Policy, 12*(2), 7–21.

Harper, S.R., Patton, L.D., & Wooden, O.S. (2009). Access and equity for African American students in higher education: A critical race historical analysis of policy efforts. *Journal of Higher Education, 80*(4), 389–414.

Haviland, V.S. (2008). "Things get glossed over": Rearticulating the silencing power of whiteness in education. *Journal of Teacher Education, 59*(1), 40–54.

Hilliard, A., Perry, T., & Steele, C. (2003). *Young, gifted, and Black: Promoting high achievement Among African-American students.* Boston, MA: Beacon.

hooks, b. (1986). Sisterhood: Political solidarity between women. *Feminist Review,* 23, 125–138.

Howard, T. (2001). Powerful pedagogy for African American students: A case of four teachers. *Urban Education, 36*(2), 179–202.

Howard, T. (2003). Culturally responsive pedagogy: Ingredients for critical teacher reflection. *Theory into Practice, 42*(3), 195–202.

Howard-Woods, C., Laidley, C., & Omidi, M. (2018). *Charlottesville: White supremacy, populism, and resistance.* New York, NY: Public Seminar Books.

Hughey, M. (2014). White backlash in the 'post-racial' United States. *Ethnic and Racial Studies, 37*(5), 721–730.

Hunter, M. (2016). Colorism in the classroom: How skin tone stratifies African American and Latina/o students. *Theory into Practice, 55*(1), 54–61.

Hylton, K. (2005). 'Race', sport and leisure: Lessons from critical race theory. *Leisure Studies, 24*(1), 81–98.

Hytten, K., & Adkins, A. (2001). Thinking through a pedagogy of whiteness. *Educational Theory, 51* (4), 433–450.

Hytten, K., & Warren, J. (2003). Engaging whiteness: How racial power gets reified in education. *International Journal of Qualitative Studies in Education, 16*(1), 65–89.

Irizarry, J. (2011). En la lucha: The struggles and triumphs of Latino/a pre-service teachers. *Teachers College Record, 113*(12), 2804–2835.

Irizarry, J., & Donaldson, M.L. (2012). Teach for America: The Latinization of U.S. schools and the critical shortage of Latina/o teachers. *American Educational Research Journal, 49*(1), 155–194.

Irvine, J.J., & Irvine, R. (2007). The impact of the desegregation process on the education of Black students: A retrospective analysis. *Journal of Negro Education, 76*(3), 297–305.

Irvine, R.W., & Irvine, J.J. (1983). The impact of the desegregation process on the education of Black students: Key variables. *The Journal of Negro Education, 52*(4), 410–422.

Jay, M. (2009). Race-ing through the school day: African American educators' experiences with race and racism in schools. *International Journal of Qualitative Studies in Education, 22*(6), 671–685.

Jennings, M.E., & Lynn, M. (2005). The house that race built: Critical pedagogy, African American education, and the re-conceptualization of critical race pedagogy. *Educational Foundations, 19*(3–4), 15–32.

Karpinski, C. (2006). Bearing the burden of desegregation: Black principals and brown. *Urban Education, 41*(3), 237–276.

Kim, L. (2001). "I was [so] busy fighting racism I didn't even know I was being oppressed as a woman!": Challenges, changes, and empowerment in teaching about women of color. *National Women's Studies Association Journal, 13*(2), 98–111.

King, E., & Butler, B.R. (2015). Who cares about diversity? A preliminary investigation of diversity exposure in teacher preparation programs. *Multicultural Perspectives, 17*, 46–52.

King, J., McIntosh, A., & Bell-Ellwanger, J. (2016). Report titled "Developmental education: Challenges and strategies for reform." Retrieved from https://www2.ed.gov/about/offices/list/opepd/education-strategies.pdf.

Kohli, R. (2008). Breaking the cycle of racism in the classroom: Critical race reflections from future teachers of color. *Teacher Education Quarterly, 35*(4), 177–188.

Kohli, R. (2009). Critical race reflections: Valuing the experiences of teachers of color in teacher education. *Race, Ethnicity and Education, 12*(2), 235–251.

Kohli, R. (2014). Unpacking internalized racism: Teachers of color striving for racially just classrooms. *Race, Ethnicity and Education, 17*(3), 367–387.

Kohli, R., & Pizarro, M. (2016). Fighting to educate our own: Teachers of color, relational accountability, and the struggle for racial justice. *Equity and Excellence in Education, 49*(1), 72–84.

Kolchin, P. (2002). The new history of race in America. *The Journal of American History, 89*(1), 154–173.

Kubota, R. (2016). The multi/plural turn, postcolonial theory, and neoliberal multiculturalism: Complicities and implications for applied linguistics. *Applied Linguistics, 37*(4), 474–494.

Kuo, J. (1998). Excluded, segregated, and forgotten: A historical view of the discrimination of Chinese Americans in public schools. *Asian Law Journal, 5,* 181–212.

Ladson-Billings, G. (1995). Toward a theory of culturally relevant pedagogy. *American Educational Research Journal, 32*(3), 465–491.

Ladson-Billings, G. (1996). Silences as weapons: Challenges of a Black professor teaching white students. *Theory into Practice, 35*(2), 79–85.

Ladson-Billings, G. (1998). Just what is critical race theory and what's it doing in a nice field like education? *International Journal of Qualitative Studies in Education, 11*(1), 7–24.

Ladson-Billings, G. (2001). *Crossing over to Canaan: The journey of new teachers crossing over into diverse classrooms.* San Francisco, CA: Jossey-Bass.

Ladson-Billings, G. (2004). Landing on the wrong note: The price we paid for brown. *Educational Researcher, 33*(7), 3–13.

Ladson-Billings, G. (2011). Asking the right questions: A research agenda for studying teacher diversity in teacher education. In A. Ball & C. Tyson (eds), *Studying diversity in teacher education* (pp. 385–398). Lanham, MD: Rowman & Littlefield Publishers.

Ladson-Billings, G. (2014). Culturally relevant pedagogy 2.0: a.k.a. the remix. *Harvard Educational Review, 84*(1), 74–84.

Ladson-Billings, G., & Tate, W.F. (1995). Toward a critical race theory in education. *Teachers College Record, 97*(1), 47–68.

Lee, S., & Walsh, D. (2017). Socially just, culturally sustaining pedagogy for diverse immigrant youth. In D. Paris & H.S. Alim (eds), *Culturally sustaining pedagogies: Teaching and learning for justice in a changing world* (pp. 191–206). New York, NY: Teachers College Press.

Leonardo, Z. (2002). The souls of white folks: Critical pedagogy, whiteness studies, and globalization discourse. *Race, Ethnicity and Education, 5*(1), 29–50.

Leonardo, Z. (2004). The color of supremacy: Beyond the discourse of 'white privilege'. *Educational Philosophy and Theory, 36*(2), 137–152.

Leonardo, Z. (2007). The war on schools: NCLB, nation creation, and the educational construction of whiteness. *Race, Ethnicity and Education, 10*(3), 261–278.

Leonardo, Z. (2009). *Race, whiteness and education.* New York, NY: Routledge.

Levine-Rasky, C. (2000a). Framing whiteness: Working through the tensions in introducing whiteness to educators. *Race, Ethnicity and Education, 3*(3), 271–292.

Levine-Rasky, C. (2000b). The practice of whiteness among teacher candidates. *International Studies in Sociology of Education, 10*(3), 263–284.

Levine-Rasky, C. (2006). Discontinuities of multiculturalism. *Canadian Ethnic Studies, 38*(3), 87–105.

Levine-Rasky, C. (2012). Critical/relational/contextual: Toward a model for studying whiteness. In C. Levine-Rasky (ed.), *Working through whiteness: International perspectives.* Albany, NY: State University of New York Press.

Levine-Rasky, C. (2016). *Whiteness fractured.* New York, NY: Routledge.

Lewis, A., Chesler, M., & Forman, T. (2000). The impact of "colorblind" ideologies on students of color: Intergroup relations at a predominantly white university. *Journal of Negro Education, 69*(1/2), 74–91.

Li, M. (2009). Is there "white flight" into private schools? New evidence from high school and beyond. *Economics of Education Review, 28*(3), 382–392.

Lipman, P. (1995). "Bringing out the best in them": The contribution of culturally relevant teachers to educational reform. *Theory into Practice, 34*(3), 202–208.

Locke, S. (2004). Reflections of Native American teacher education on Bear Ridge. *The Rural Educator, 26*(1), 15–23.

Lopez, G. (2003). The (racially neutral) politics of education: A critical race theory perspective. *Education Administration Quarterly, 39*(1), 68–94.

Love, B.J. (2004). *Brown* plus 50 counter-storytelling: A critical race theory analysis of the "majoritarian achievement gap" story. *Equity and Excellence in Education, 37*(3), 227–246.

Macdonald, V.M., & Monkman, K. (2005). Setting the context: Historical perspectives on Latino/a education. In P. Pedraza & M. Rivera (eds), *Latino education: An agenda for community Action Research* (pp. 47–74). Mahwah, NJ: Lawrence Erlbaum Associates Publishers.

Malin, N. (ed.). (2000). *Professionalism, boundaries and the workplace*. London: Routledge.

Matias, C.E. (2013a). On the "Flip" side: A teacher educator of color unveiling the dangerous minds of white teacher candidates. *Teacher Education Quarterly, 40*(2), 53–73.

Matias, C.E. (2013b). Check yo' self before you wreck yo' self and our kids: Counterstories from culturally responsive white teachers...to culturally responsive white teachers! *Interdisciplinary Journal of Teaching and Learning, 3*(2), 68–81.

Matias, C.E. (2013c). Who you callin' white?! A critical counter-story on colouring white identity. *Race Ethnicity and Education, 16*(3), 291–315.

Matias, C.E. (2016). "Why do you make me hate myself?": Re-teaching Whiteness, abuse, and love in urban teacher education. *Teaching Education, 27*(2), 194–211.

Matias, C.E., & Liou, D. (2015). Tending to the heart of communities of color: Towards critical race teacher activism. *Urban Education, 50*(5), 601–625.

Matias, C.E., & Mackey (2016). Breakin' down whiteness in antiracist teaching: Introducing critical whiteness pedagogy. *The Urban Review, 48*(1), 32–50.

Matias, C.E., & Newlove, P. (2017). Better the devil you see, than the one you don't: Bearing witness to emboldened en-whitening epistemology in the Trump era. *International Journal of Qualitative Studies in Education, 30*(10), 920–928.

Matias, C.E., & Nishi, N. (2018). ParentCrit epilog. *International Journal of Qualitative Studies in Education, 31*(1), 82–85.

Matias, C.E, Viesca, K., Garrison-Wade, D., Tandon, M., & Galindo, R. (2014). "What is critical whiteness doing in OUR nice field like critical race theory?" Applying CRT and CWS to understand the white imaginations of white teacher candidates. *Equity and Excellence in Education, 47*(3), 289–304.

Matthews, J. (2002). An ambitious juncture: Racism and the formation of Asian femininity. *Australian Feminist Studies, 17*(38), 207–219.

McCarty, T., & Lee, T. (2014). Critical culturally sustaining/revitalizing pedagogy and indigenous education sovereignty. *Harvard Educational Review, 84*(1), 101–124.

McGee, E.O., Alvarez, A., & Milner IV, H.R. (2016). Colorism as a salient space for understanding in teacher preparation. *Theory into Practice, 55*(1), 69–79.

McIntyre, A. (1997). *Making meaning of whiteness: Exploring racial identity with white teachers*. Albany, NY: State University of NY Press.

McLaren, P. (1998). Revolutionary pedagogy in post-revolutionary times: Rethinking the political economy of critical education. *Educational theory, 48*(4), 431–462.

Milner, H.R. (2006). The promise of Black teachers' success with Black students. *Educational Foundations, 20,* 89–104.

Milner, H.R. (2008). Critical race theory and interest convergence as analytic tools in teacher education policies and practice. *Journal of Teacher Education, 59*(4), 332–346.

Milner, H.R. (2011). Culturally relevant pedagogy in a diverse urban classroom. *The Urban Review, 43*(1), 66–89.

Milner, H.R. (2013). Analyzing poverty, learning, and teaching through a critical race theory lens. *Review of Research in Education, 37*(1), 1–53.

Milner, H.R. (2017). Where's the race in culturally relevant pedagogy? *Teachers College Record, 119*(1), 1–33.

Milner, H.R., & Howard, T. (2004). Black teachers, Black students, Black communities, and brown: Perspectives and insights from experts. *Journal of Negro Education, 73*(3), 285–297.

Milner, H.R., Pearman, F., & McGee, E. (2013). Critical race theory, interest convergence, and teacher education. In M. Lynn & A.D. Dixson (eds), *Handbook of critical race theory in education* (pp. 339–354). New York, NY: Routledge.

Mitchell, K. (2013). Race, difference, meritocracy, and English: Majoritarian stories in the education of secondary multilingual learners. *Race, Ethnicity and Education, 16*(3), 339–364.

Modica, M. (2015). Unpacking the 'colorblind approach': Accusations of racism at a friendly, mixed-race school. *Race, Ethnicity and Education, 18*(3), 396–418.

Mogadime, D. (2008). Racial differential experiences of employment equity for women teachers: One teacher's narrative of resistance and struggle. *Journal of Black Studies, 39*(1), 85–108.

Morris, J.E. (2001). Forgotten voices of African American educators: Critical race perspectives on the implementation of a desegregation plan. *Educational Policy, 15*(4), 575–600.

Morris, J.E. (2004). Can anything good come from Nazareth? Race, class, and African American schooling and community in the urban South and Midwest. *American Educational Research Journal, 41*(1), 69–112.

Morrison, G.Z. (2008). Two separate worlds: Students of color at a predominantly white university. *Journal of Black Studies, 40*(5), 987–1010.

National Center for Education Statistics (2017). *A quarter century of changes in the elementary and secondary teaching force: From 1987 to 2012.* Retrieved from https://nces.ed.gov/pubs2017/2017092.pdf.

National Center for Education Statistics (2018a). *The condition of education 2018.* Retrieved from https://nces.ed.gov/pubsearch/pubsinfo.asp?pubid=2018144.

National Center for Education Statistics (2018b). *Characteristics of traditional public schools and public charter schools.* Retrieved from https://nces.ed.gov/programs/coe/indicator_cla.asp.

National Collaborative on Diversity in the Teaching Force. (2004). *Assessment of diversity in America's Teaching Force: A call to action.* Washington, DC: Author.

Nettles, M., Scatton, L., Steinberg, J., & Tyler, L. (2011). *Performance and passing rate differences of African American and white prospective teachers on Praxis examinations.* Princeton, NJ: Educational Testing Service.

O'Connor, K.E. (2008). "You choose to care": Teachers, emotions and professional identity. *Teaching and Teacher Education, 24*(1), 117–126.

Orfield, G., Ee, J., Frankenburg, E., & Siegel-Hawley, G. (2016). *Brown* at 62: School segregation by race, poverty, and state. *The Civil Rights Project,* UCLA, Los Angeles, CA.

Osgood, J. (2010). Reconstructing professionalism in ECEC: The case for the 'critically reflective emotional professional.' *An International Research Journal, 30*(2), 119–133.

Paris, D. (2012). Culturally sustaining pedagogy: A needed change in stance, terminology, and practice. *Educational Researcher, 41*(3), 93–97.

Paris, D., & Alim, H.S. (2014). What are we seeking to sustain with culturally sustaining pedagogy? A loving critique forward. *Harvard Educational Review, 84*(1), 85–100.

Paris, D., & Alim, H.S. (2017). *Culturally sustaining pedagogies: Teaching and learning for justice in a changing world.* New York, NY: Teachers College Press.

Parker, L. (2019). *Race is…race isn't: Critical race theory and qualitative Studies in education.* New York, NY: Routledge.

Perez Huber, L., Johnson, R.N., & Kohli, R. (2006). Naming racism: A conceptual look at internalized racism in US schools. *Chicana/o Latina/o Law Review,* 26, 183–206.

Petchauer, E. (2012). Teacher licensure exams and Black teacher candidates: Toward new theory and promising practice. *The Journal of Negro Education, 81*(3), 252–267.

Phoenix, A. (2009). De-colonizing practices: Negotiating narratives from racialised and gendered experiences of education. *Race, Ethnicity and Education, 12*(1), 101–114.

Phoenix, A., & Pattynama, P. (2006). Intersectionality. *European Journal of Women's Studies, 13*(3), 187–192.

Powell, R. (1997). Then the beauty emerges: A longitudinal case study of culturally relevant teaching. *Teaching and Teacher Education, 13*(5), 467–484.

Powers, J.M. (2008). Forgotten history: Mexican American school segregation in Arizona from 1900-1951. *Equity and Excellence in Education, 41*(4), 467–481.

Puigvert, L. (2003). Equality of differences. In E. Beck-Gernsheim, J. Butler, & L. Puigvert (eds), *Women and social transformation* (pp. 99–115). New York, NY: Peter Lang Publishing.

Raible, J., & Irizarry, J.G. (2010). Redirecting the teacher's gaze: Teacher education, youth surveillance, and the school-to-prison pipeline. *Teaching and Teacher Education, 26*(5), 1196–1203.

Reardon, S.F., & Yun, J.T. (2002). Private school racial enrollments and segregation. *The Civil Rights Project* report. Cambridge, MA: Harvard University.

Reardon, S.F., & Yun, J.T. (2003). Integrating neighborhoods, segregating schools: The retreat from school segregation in the South. *North Carolina Law Review, 81,* 1563–1595.

Renzulli, L.A., & Evans, L. (2005). School choice, charter schools, and white flight. *Social Problems, 52*(3), 398–418.

Renzulli, L.A., Parrott, H.M., & Beattie, I.R. (2011). Racial mismatch and school type: Teacher satisfaction and retention in charter and traditional public schools. *Sociology of Education, 84*(1), 23–48.

Rodriguez, D. (2011). Silent rage and the politics of resistance: Countering seductions of whiteness and the road to politicization and empowerment. *Qualitative Inquiry, 17*(7), 589–598.

Rogers, R., & Mosley, M. (2006). Racial literacy in a second-grade classroom: Critical race theory, whiteness studies, and literacy research. *Reading Research Quarterly, 41*(4), 462–495.

Rogers-Ard, R., Knaus, C.B., Epstein, K.K., & Mayfield, K. (2013). Racial diversity sounds nice; Systems transformation? Not so much: Developing urban teachers of color. *Urban Education, 48*(3), 451–479.

Rollock, N. (2012). The invisibility of race: Intersectional reflections on the liminal space of alterity. *Race, Ethnicity and Education, 15*(1), 65–84.

Rong, X.L., & Preissle, J. (1997). The continuing decline in Asian American teachers. *American Educational Research Journal, 34*(2), 267–293.

Salinas, C. (2000). El Colegio Altamirano (1897–1958): New histories of Chicano education in the Southwest. *The Educational Forum, 65,* 80–86.

San Pedro, T. (2018). Abby as ally: An argument for culturally disrupting pedagogy. *American Educational Research Journal, 55*(6), 1193–1232.

Siddle Walker, E.V. (2000). Valued segregated schools for African American children in the South, 1935–1969: A review of common themes and characteristics. *Review of Educational Research, 70*(3), 253–286.

Simon, M., & Azzarito, L. (2018). "Singled out because of skin color": Exploring ethnic minority female teachers' embodiment in physical education. *Sport, Education and Society, 24*(2), 105–120.

Simon, M., & Azzarito, L. (2019). "Putting blinders on": Ethnic minority female PE teachers' identity struggles negotiating racialized discourses. *Journal of Teaching in Physical Education, 38*(4), 367–376.

Sleeter, C. (2001). Preparing teachers for culturally diverse schools: Research and the overwhelming presence of whiteness. *Journal of Teacher Education, 52*(2), 94–106.

Sleeter, C. (2016) Wrestling with problematics of whiteness in teacher education. *International Journal of Qualitative Studies in Education, 29*(8), 1065–1068.

Sleeter, C. (2017). Critical race theory and the whiteness of teacher education. *Urban Education, 52*(2), 155–169.

Smith-Maddox, R., & Solórzano, D.G. (2002). Using critical race theory, Paulo Freire's problem-posing method, and case study research to confront race and racism in education. *Qualitative Inquiry, 8*(1), 66–84.

Solem, M., Lee, J., & Schempler, B. (2009). Departmental climate and students experiences in graduate geography programs. *Research in Higher Education, 50*(3), 268–292.

Solomona, R.P., Portelli, J., Daniel, B.J., & Campbell, A. (2005). The discourse of denial: How white teacher candidates construct race, racism, and 'white privilege.' *Race, Ethnicity and Education, 8*(2), 147–169.

Solórzano, D. (1998). Critical race theory, race and gender microaggressions, and the experience of Chicana and Chicano scholars. *Qualitative Studies in Education, 11*(1), 121–136.

Solórzano, D., & Bernal, D. (2001). Examining transformational resistance through a critical race and LatCrit theory and framework: Chicana and Chicano students in an urban context. *Urban Education, 36*(3), 308–342.

Solórzano, D.G., Ceja, M., & Yosso, T. (2000). Critical race theory, racial microaggressions, and campus climate: The experiences of African American college students. *Journal of Negro Education, 69*(1/2), 60–73.

Solórzano, D.G., & Solórzano, R.W. (1995). The Chicano educational experience: A framework for effective schools in Chicano communities. *Educational Policy, 9*(3), 293–314.

Solórzano, D.G., & Yosso, T.J. (2001). Critical race and LatCrit theory and method: Counter-storytelling. *International Journal of Qualitative Studies in Education, 14*(4), 471–495.

Solórzano, D.G., & Yosso, T.J. (2002). A critical race counterstory of race, racism, and affirmative action. *Equity and Excellence in Education, 35*(2), 155–168.

Souto-Manning, M., & Mitchell, C. (2010). The role of action research in fostering culturally responsive practices in a preschool classroom. *Early Childhood Education Journal, 37*(4), 269–277.

Steele, C.M. (2011). *Whistling Vivaldi: How stereotypes affect us and what we can do*. New York, NY: Norton & Company.

Tate, W.F. (1997). Critical race theory and education: History, theory, and implications. *Review of Research in Education, 22*(1), 195–247.

Tatum, B.D. (2017). *Why are all the Black kids sitting together in the cafeteria? And other conversations about race*. New York, NY: Basic Books.

Tejeda, C., Espinoza, M., & Gutierrez, K. (2003). Toward a decolonizing pedagogy: Social justice reconsidered. In P. Trifonas (ed.), *Pedagogies of difference: Rethinking education for social change* (pp. 10–40). New York, NY: RoutledgeFalmer.

Teranishi, R. (2004). Yellow and Brown: Emerging Asian American populations and residential segregation. *Equity and Excellence in Education, 37*(3), 255–263.

Tillman, L. (2004). (Un)intended consequences? The impact of the *Brown v. Board of Education* decision on the employment status of Black educators. *Education and Urban Society, 36*(3), 280–303.

Unger, R.M. (1983). The critical legal studies movement. *Harvard Law Review, 96*(3), 561–674.

U.S. Department of Education (2016). Report titled "The state of racial diversity in the educator workforce." Retrieved from https://www2.ed.gov/rschstat/eval/higher ed/racial-diversity/state-racial-diversity-workforce.pdf.

U.S. Government Accountability Office (2016). Report t titled "K-12 Education: Better use of information could help agencies identify disparities and address racial discrimination." Retrieved from https://www.gao.gov/products/GAO-16-345.

Ward, J. (1996). Raising resisters: The role of truth telling in the psychological development of African American girls. In B. Leadbetter & N. Way (eds), *Urban girls: Resisting stereotypes, creating identities* (pp. 85–99). New York: New York University Press.

White, M. (2002). Paradise lost? Teachers' perspectives on the use of cultural capital in the segregated schools of New Orleans, Louisiana. *The Journal of African American History, 87*(2), 269–281.

Williams, E., Graham, A., McCary-Henderson, S., & Floyd, L. (2009). "From where I stand": African American teacher candidates on their decision to teach. *The Educational Forum, 73*(4), 348–364.

Winans, A.E. (2012). Cultivating critical emotional literacy: Cognitive and contemplative approaches to engaging difference. *College English, 75*(2), 150–170.

Yosso, T., Smith, W., Ceja, M., & Solórzano, D.G. (2009). Critical race theory, racial microaggressions, and campus racial climate for Latina/o undergraduates. *Harvard Education Review, 79*(4), 659–691.

Yosso, T.J. (2002). Toward a critical race curriculum. *Equity and Excellence in Education, 35*(2), 93–107.

Yosso, T.J. (2005). Whose culture has capital? A critical race theory discussion of community cultural wealth. *Race, Ethnicity and Education, 8*(1), 69–91.

Yosso, T.J., Parker, L., Solórzano, D., & Lynn, M. (2004). From Jim Crow to affirmative action and back again: A critical race discussion of racialized rationales and access to higher education. *Review of Research in Education, 28,* 1–25.

Young, E. (2010). Challenges to conceptualizing and actualizing culturally relevant pedagogy: How visible is theory in classroom practice? *Journal of Teacher Education, 61*(3), 248–260.

Index

affirmative action, 28, 30–31, 33, 62
agency, 6–7, 38, 70, 74–75, 86–87, 96,
   98, 107, 114–16
Ahmed, S., 117–18
Alim, H.S., 112
Allen, K.M., 107
Allen, Q., 115
Allen, R.L., 45
American dream, 86
American way, 45
Amos, Y.T., 23
API. *See* Asian and Pacific Island (API)
Aronson, B., 113
Asian American teachers, 2
Asian and Pacific Island (API):
   immigrants, 14; populations, 14;
   students, 14; teachers, 14
assimilation practices, 85

bachelor-degree seeking college
   students, 2
Baez, B., 114
*Bakke vs Regents of the University of
   California* ruling, 31
Balf, R., 107
bearing witness, 75, 80–81, 84, 87, 96
Bell, D.A., 65
Berry, T.R., 115
Black communities, 25
Black principals, 20, 24

Black teachers, 2, 18–20, 24–25, 36, 59,
   77–78, 80, 83, 101, 115
Bonilla-Silva, E., 6, 54–56
Borrero, N.E., 107
Brown, M.C., 116
Brown II rulings (1955), 16
Brown rulings, 9–10, 12, 14–19,
   21–22, 23–27, 30, 32–33, 65;
   early forerunners, 17; failures, 18;
   racial equality, 15; unanticipated
   consequence of, 19; white interest
   convergence, 16
Brown vs Board of Education rulings, 6,
   58, 65, 115

Caruthers, L., 107
Chinese Exclusion Act (1882), 11
Chinese immigrant parents, 77
Citizens Council, 16
Civil Rights Act (1968), 30
Civil Rights Movement, 19–21, 36, 56,
   58–59, 67
Civil War, 28
CLS. *See* critical legal scholarship (CLS)
Cochran-Smith, M., 107
Cold War, 16, 65, 92
colorblind approach, 26, 58, 67
colorblind educational landscape, 36
colorblind perspective, legitimization
   of, 44

About the Authors

Mara Simon is an assistant professor of teacher education at Springfield College. Before transitioning to her role in higher education, she was an elementary school teacher in New York City for nine years. She graduated with her educational doctorate (Ed.D.) from Teachers College, Columbia University in 2018. As a scholar and educator committed to social justice research and pedagogy, she has authored book chapters and articles exploring the embodied identities and lived experiences of teachers of color, along with identifying issues of racial inequity in education and highlighting the need for critical pedagogy. She is the recipient of multiple awards from national field organizations for her work, both as a doctoral student and an early career scholar. Mara currently resides in Massachusetts with her spouse and two children.

Laura Azzarito is a professor of physical culture and education. She is also program director of the graduate program in physical culture and physical education pedagogy, and co-director of the Visual Research Center for Education, Art, and Social Change at Teachers College, Columbia University, United States. Her research focuses on understanding nuanced conceptualizations of young people's embodiment with attention to the complex articulation of gender/sex, race/ethnicity, (dis)ability, and social class. Professor Azzarito has several books published: *Social Justice in Globalized Fitness and Health: Bodies out of Sight*; *Pedagogies, Physical Culture, and Visual Methods* (with David Kirk); and *"Race," Youth Sport, Physical Activity and Health. Global Perspectives* (with Symeon Dagkas and Kevin Hylton).

Made in United States
North Haven, CT
02 June 2023

37263255R00090